P & P

Educating Older People

SECOND EDITION

M. F. CLEUGH

TAVISTOCK PUBLICATIONS

First published in 1962
by Tavistock Publications Limited
11 New Fetter Lane, London E.C.4
First published as a Social Science
Paperback in 1970
Printed in Great Britain
by photolithography
by The Camelot Press Ltd
London and Southampton

SBN 422 75130 8

35470
6001286876
35470

05

Distributed in the U.S.A. by
Barnes & Noble, Inc.

CONTENTS

FOREWORD TO THE SECOND EDITION

SINCE THIS BOOK first appeared I have been asked on a number of occasions to talk about the running of discussions in education, youth work, and the social services. A frequent question is 'How do you get *everybody* to take part?' and the unspoken assumption seems to be that something is wrong if a single individual remains silent to the end of even one meeting. This seems to me an unnecessary worry, especially when discussions are contrasted with the usual lecture situation where a total silence doesn't seem to bother anybody, and so it may be worth while to repeat that, provided there is reasonably good general participation, the tutor can rest content, and that he will lose more than he is likely to gain if he chivvies the silent and the shy into joining in before they feel ready.

A more important difficulty concerns some very strange, and to my mind thoroughly unsound, ideas that are current regarding the study of group processes. I will summarize them as follows:

Anxiety and pain are an integral part of group experience.

Relations among group members are of necessity frequently strained, with a good deal of scapegoating going on.

An angry argument is to be welcomed as a sign of depth and commitment.

We can learn best how groups function by setting up groups that have nothing to do other than study themselves.

Interpretation is essential.

My experience in the last twenty years in running discussion groups has led me to very different conclusions, which I had an opportunity to state in an article in *Forum* (1968). I am grateful to the Editor for permission to use the material now. Although these conclusions can only be stated baldly here, they are not merely dogmas and I can document them.

Anxiety and pain occur. They must be faced. They must not be unnecessarily increased or stimulated. Group learning is primarily a joyful process. Release, energy, and insight are the primary experiences: anxiety and pain are secondary.

Learning takes place rapidly in a friendly group: scape-goating is rare, and its occurrence need not be regarded with complacency, but on the contrary as a sign of lack of skill in the leader.

Expression of deep feeling is more likely to occur in a setting of trust, confidence, and security. Surface fireworks get nowhere and the entertainment they afford is trivial. Unaccept-able feelings, including aggressive ones, need to be expressed – and accepted: but their frequency and violence are not a barometer of the depth of issues tackled by the group.

A group that has nothing to do is an abnormal group. (Comparison: studying digestion in a body which has nothing to eat!) All normal groups have tasks to perform: as they get on with them, mechanisms are brought into play and these can be studied in retrospect. Some members become interested in the processes of group learning and spontaneously examine them for themselves with considerable insight and without anxiety. Others do not gain this, second-order, insight, but they have benefited at the primary level from the achievement of their learning task. This seems to me sounder educationally than dragging everyone through by the scruff of their necks beyond their level of comprehension, emotional as well as intellectual.

Interpretation, far from being essential, is nearly always

either useless or harmful. Is it not, in essence, a claim to play God? It is my contention that the process of interpretation involves a contradiction with the expressed aims of group study that is not merely a surface inconsistency: this contradiction reappears at the second level, and the third, and the fourth, to an infinite regress – in short it is fundamental.

Let us imagine a very skilled consultant, whose interpretations are always dead right (a tall order! but let it pass) and analyse the implications of his activities at the receiving end. If these are shown to be unhelpful, even though he is in fact right, then *a fortiori* there is still less to be said for the inaccurate, the biased, and the erratic interpreter.

Interpretation is always threatening. It involves piercing defences that have been erected to guard tender spots. There is all the world of difference between the voluntary dropping of defences in a situation of trust, and having them forcibly penetrated. The latter appears aggressive, ruthless, threatening: the defences become more, not less, necessary. If you know that comments will be made on the 'meaning' of your behaviour, the obvious reaction is to mobilize your defences and retire behind them; they are going to be needed. So the person retreats, and shows only what is trivial. The consultant claims godlike omniscience and by so doing devalues the creatures wriggling in front of him of their humanity. He *knows*, and he will tell them what he knows, willy-nilly. He is the authoritarian par excellence. So it is no good talking piously about a 'climate of acceptance', or a 'non-judgemental' attitude to the group, or 'encouraging the expression of repressed feeling' – the reality is other, it is an authoritarian, non-reversible situation, and there is the fundamental contradiction.

In my experience I have plenty of evidence for advocating the eschewal of interpretative comment. In groups where there genuinely is a climate of acceptance and a non-judgemental attitude, people are left unmolested. They can join in or be silent. They can learn to challenge ideas without attacking people, and, equally, learn to accept challenge without its becoming a personal threat to be countered aggressively. There is a lot of fun to be had from the comradeship of a harmonious working group. It is safe to express feelings spontaneously. Defences that are not needed against unwelcome invasions of personal privacy tend to drop. Discussions become more genuinely self-involving, and may reach considerable depth, but easily and gaily – in contrast to the exchange of barren trivialities, punctuated by explosions, of the defence-ridden interpretative groups.

In sum, I would rest my contention against interpretation on three counts – it is authoritarian, it is bad-mannered, it is futile.

An exchange of assertion and counter-assertion accomplishes little. I have written this because I did not want the case to go by default while the opposite views become the orthodoxy in spite of their manifest shortcomings. But what is really needed is more evidence in the form of full transcripts of proceedings in discussion groups, and these are not easily come by. Is there any reason for this shyness? Why should we be fobbed off with large claims of 'great depth', 'significant learnings', etc., and a general tone of mystique and long words, when the actual examples given are brief and of a startling and humourless banality? I have myself given full examples of group discussion both in this book (Chapter 4) and in the *Institute of Education Bulletin* (1964); and of process of change in Chapters 8, 9, and 10. Please will those who dislike the views I have expressed here do the same?

M.C.

20.5.70

7

FOREWORD TO THE FIRST EDITION

In this book I have tried to be specific and to give detailed examples wherever possible: this has obvious advantages in vividness, and the reader may rephrase the examples and situations in terms of the particular setting he knows best. I have also tried to go behind the particular to the general, and to discuss issues and principles which have application over a wide field of management and of education, so that the scope of the book is not circumscribed by the provenance of the examples.

It is pleasant to acknowledge the help of those colleagues and friends whose faith in the value of the undertaking encouraged me to persevere, and also of many former students who co-operated in ways which are evident in the text. I would especially like to thank Mr. R. C. Ablewhite, Mrs. A. Benham, Dr. C. M. Fleming, Miss K. L. Hanks, and Miss L. Mickleburgh, all of whom read the manuscript, and gave valuable suggestions and criticisms. To the last named of these, who in the tenth decade of life is still interested in education, this book is dedicated, with respect and affection.

M.C.
Whittington, Salop.

Chapter One

INTRODUCTION

THIS BOOK is not about 'adult education' as the phrase is usually interpreted. I am not concerned to discuss what part can or should be played by Trade Unions, extra-mural departments of universities, local and central government, voluntary organizations such as Women's Institutes, and the host of other claimants, nor how their various activities shape or fail to shape an integrated pattern. Still less am I concerned with administration, finance, or buildings. My aim is much simpler: to consider how the educative process works when its subjects are not young persons but older ones, not willing or unwilling prisoners but voluntary contractors, not green twigs but sturdy and often unbending timber – are, in short, adults with a formed outlook on life, family responsibilities, a wealth of past experience, favourable or unfavourable, and special interests, training, or expertise. Much of what I say will be coloured by my particular experience as a tutor of adults in an advanced university course, and the examples will naturally tend to be taken from that or similar fields, but I believe that a discussion of methods and objectives can have relevance in a wider context; and that the reader who is concerned with, say, Workers' Educational Association tutoring, or the fostering of discussion groups in community centres, or the training of prison officers, may also find something of interest and use to him, after allowance is made for very different circumstances.

9

Whatever the context, adult education is of necessity concerned with the interrelations between individuals in groups, and with changes in the individuals themselves – these provide the two main divisions for the chapters that follow.

In every group, whatever the purpose, certain problems recur – problems of selection, range, social cohesion or disruption, 'tone' and atmosphere, assimilation (both of new members and of new information), the mechanics of learning, and many others. Take, for example, the question of range. The members of any group will presumably be homogeneous in one respect, that of interest in their chosen field – whether it be education in overseas territories, community development, methods of disciplining prisoners, or how to teach handicrafts in Women's Institutes – but they will be heterogeneous in all else. Some of the variations can be ignored as irrelevant to the declared purpose of the group, and others can be minimized to some extent by selection (at the same time as one selects for A, one is also cutting down the *possible* variations in B and C in so far as they are correlated with A, thus forming a cluster or pattern – the 'sergeant-major' type, for example). Nevertheless, enough variety remains to be a source of difficulty and misunderstanding, and on the other hand of richness. Individual differences within the group can be neglected by the leader only at his peril. How can he harness them so that they are not disruptive but valuable? How can he provide a setting within which each can learn at his own level? Granted that some are progressing much faster than others, how can he prevent undesirable rivalries and anxieties from emerging? Questions such as these enter into every situation of adult learning, whatever its context. Furthermore, in those situations where a definite standard has to be reached (Is she good enough to instruct others in needlework? Is he likely to make a satisfactory probation officer?), the range of ability may be such that not all the candidates can reach that standard. What is the effect of this uncertainty, both on individuals and on the group as a whole?

Selection assumes a greater purport when there is a possibility, however remote, of inability to satisfy the examiners at the end of a course.

It will be seen, even in this brief and desultory raising of questions, that they ramify. Problems of range cannot be placed in a neat compartment by themselves: they are inter-related with the need for selection, the importance of 'tone' in dispelling factions, the mechanics of learning (is a lecture the best way of imparting information to a widely varying audience?); even the distinction between group and individual problems breaks down (anxiety is infectious). Nevertheless, a start has to be made somewhere and, however artificial the division of topics, there must be one. I propose, therefore, to begin with matters that concern the group as a whole – methods of learning, the slow accretion of group feeling, stan-dards of work, leadership, and the like; and later to turn to the individuals who make up those groups – What is a real ex-perience for them? What do we mean by contact? To what extent are the attitudes of adults modifiable? Is change super-ficial or can it be more lasting? What part does confidence play?

Underlying all these is the fundamental question of aim: what is it that we are trying to do in our work with adults? The ostensible purposes of those who join groups and of those who lead them are as manifold as the titles of the courses, but the common aim of all is improvement. The skill involved may be peripheral and its development may afford only mild pleasure and satisfaction, or it may be vital to one's professional or personal development. In the latter case much more is at stake, and failure to satisfy oneself even more than failure to satisfy an external criterion can be damaging, perhaps deeply so: but small successes and gains in self-mastery and self-knowledge are correspondingly valuable.

If the certificate of attendance or performance, proudly displayed on the wall or lying forgotten in a drawer, is the sole outcome of a course of training or instruction, then, however 'successful' the experience may have seemed at the time, it can hardly be considered to have been truly educative; but if it leads beyond itself, it may be like the grain of mustard seed. A realization of the value of time is essential for all of us who work in education: quick results are not always lasting and the test of our work is to be found, not in the immediate balance-sheet of an examination pass list, but in the activities of our students over the years ahead. If they are supported and sustained, in however small a measure, by the skills they have learned and made part of themselves (whether these skills be in the field of professional knowledge, artistic expression, technical expertise, or personal or spiritual understanding), then the efforts of their teachers have been justified. The precise field is relatively unimportant, and it is in the belief that the elements which are common to many adult groups can be profitably examined that this book has been written.

In what follows, I have drawn heavily on opinions expressed by a number of my former students. These opinions are not always unanimous, and I have sometimes deliberately included conflicting ones to give an idea of range. An explanatory 'F.S.' is added at the end of direct quotations from these men and women, unless the context makes their provenance clear: other quotations are acknowledged in the usual manner.

Chapter Two

GETTING THINGS GOING

THE ANTICIPATIONS with which a number of adults enter upon a course of training will vary with their previous experience but in one respect adult students are alike – they have all had experience of schooling and think they know what it is like to learn. Some may come confidently, knowing that their 'memory' is good and that they can produce an acceptable fair copy of what has been said to them, others may be apprehensive for the opposite reason. In all cases, they are expecting from the new experience what they have found to hold good in past learning situations – it will be difficult, easy, challenging, anxiety-producing, interesting, a dull grind, or just good fun. Others in the group will be seen as intimidating in their omniscience, as fellow-sufferers in misfortune, as dangerous competitors, as comrades and possible friends, as captive audiences for showing off, or just as a blurred background. So they come, with attitudes already entrenched and expectations to some extent formed. These expectations may or may not be well founded – for example, it may *not* be sufficient just to produce an acceptable rehash of the tutor's lectures, and the confidence of one and the fears of another may soon melt away – but such as they are, they have to be taken into account. Furthermore, what are the leader's expectations as he meets his new groups? Does he perceive *them* as captive audiences for showing off? If so, they will probably remain just as vague a background as they necessarily appear at the beginning. If he is somewhat insecure himself, he may fear that they will catch him out in an inaccuracy, or aggressively challenge his position, or fail to learn as much as he hopes that they will.

When we put the two sides together – the tutor's perception of the group and the members' varying points of view regarding each other and regarding him – we have the starting-point for our discussion. Quite a complicated one!

To begin with, it is easier to take the tutor as a constant and inquire what steps he can take to set the group at its ease, establish a friendly climate, and initiate purposeful activities. At a later stage it will be necessary to see in what ways and for what reasons the leader may fail in leadership, but here let us assume that he knows what he is doing and does it reasonably well.

'Make sure that they have plenty to do at the beginning' was the advice given by an older colleague to a new tutor on his first day, and it is very sound. The present vogue for orientation courses, for gradual induction into the mysteries of whatever-it-may-be, suffers from the disadvantage that a fatal appearance of tentativeness may be given. It is not necessary to explain everything at the beginning on the (mistaken) assumption that the new students have only to receive a logical explanation of the principles on which the course is planned for it to assume as neat a pattern in their minds as it has in the tutor's mind. On the contrary, too much explanation may defeat its own end and leave confusion worse confounded. It is safer to assume that very little will be comprehended from the first crowded day or evening in new surroundings, and better to leave the students with one clear idea of what it is they are going to do at the next meeting of the group, than with a confused impression, such as is expressed in, 'We heard a great deal but I couldn't get it straight somehow. Oh dear, I'm afraid it's all going to be very hard.' In the latter case, all they are learning is that perhaps they are not going to be equal to the course after all – and they may turn up in the wrong place next time.

There is a lot to be said for starting *in medias res* – not with the logical structure of the subject, which may seem academic and remote to adults, but with their avowed interest in actual situations or problems. Undergraduates may submit, with protest, to 'starting off with the skeleton', but adults who attend a psychology class expect a meatier introduction – the bony structure of logic attracts them less than flesh and blood. (Of course this does not mean that work should *remain* at the level of superficial problems. As Peers (1958, p. 223) said, 'The attempt to discuss "problems" without the support of the accumulated heritage of past knowledge . . . will lead nowhere. There can be no short cuts in adult education'; and he called for 'the progressive building up of a body of related facts'. What I am concerned with here is the starting-point.)

As an example, the first assignment may be a piece of practical work or a visit of observation, which can give a lead for discussion at the next meeting of the group and help people in getting to know each other. Another possibility, where the nature of the course and the size of the group permit it, is to begin by asking the members to say what topics they hope will be covered, list these, and perhaps make an immediate plunge into one of them. Not all suggestions will be suitable or practicable, some may need to be taken up later, others not at all; and the tutor will have to decide quickly which is the best starting-point. It will probably be found that this first snap discussion is ragged and desultory, and tends to wander into irrelevancy. If the tutor has a tidy mind, he may be rather appalled by the lack of sequence and wonder whether he ought to intervene. But if the discussion is going at all, he may be better advised to refrain, and feel relieved that the situation is not one of blank silence where he is *forced* to intervene.

After the discussion is over, when he reflects on what has been achieved, he may feel 'Nothing – it will all have to be done again'; and so it will, unless he has been exceptionally fortunate. But that does not mean that the time has been wasted, if he considers the following points:

1. A start has been made in introducing the members to each other. It is partial, in that some have not joined in, but those who have participated have probably enjoyed themselves.
2. A certain amount of tension has been relaxed.
3. The tutor is beginning to learn something about how his group is constituted. Individuals emerge from the blur of faces and he may wisely seize the opportunity to learn names as soon as possible.

These are fairly obvious considerations, but he may profitably carry his reflections further.

1. Is it in fact true that nothing has been learned by the students, even though the ostensible subject has not been advanced? The impression they are likely to carry away with them is that their contributions have been asked for and presumably will be welcomed when they feel able to join in, even if during this first meeting they have been silent. This impression, if reinforced by subsequent experiences, is itself a most important piece of learning, since it can have a snow-ball effect. It is more important for a student to learn to feel that he himself has something to offer to promote the common effort than to fill his notebook with neat facts or diagrams. The latter he will have to memorize, but the former he is learning without conscious effort and it will stand him in good stead later. Unconscious social learning should be taken into account as well as manifest content.
2. Furthermore, it is no bad thing if the students begin to appreciate that active effort from themselves is required and not just passive absorption of whatever pabulum is put before them. This does not imply that these ideas can be implanted overnight and are then safely assimilated. On the contrary, their assimilation will probably be a long process, particularly

when former attitudes and expectations have been very different.

3. 'Start where the learner is' is a fundamental principle of teaching and is as true of adults as of children. It may be disconcerting to the earnest tutor, who has started off with high expectations of what he is going to accomplish with his group, to find that his expectations were pitched too high. But if in fact the tutor is unrealistic, it is better that he discover this as soon as possible. There is no better way than discussion to find out at what level his students are actually functioning; then his only sensible response is to accept the finding and begin at that level, otherwise he and his group will be permanently at cross purposes.

I would suggest, therefore, that a preliminary group discussion of this sort can be most useful, almost irrespective of its apparent outcome. It can help people to get to know one another and, on a deeper level, it enables both the group members and the leader to set their sights more accurately. It goes without saying that these preliminary impressions will need to be reinforced as time goes on; but the process of adjustment has started, and that is the main thing.

So far, I have mentioned practical work and, at rather more length, discussion in the initial stages of the course. Next, it will be well to deal with the periods devoted to set instruction. This can be done briefly, since many of the points already touched on still apply.

Early lectures should be relatively straightforward. They should not be thought of by the tutor as opportunities for erudite display, nor should they plunge into a mass of detail, however interesting, where some students may lose sight of the wood for the trees. On the other hand, it is a mistake to go to the opposite extreme of giving only an abstract framework, which has logical but not psychological priority. The middle way is to find, if possible, an uncomplicated topic, whose interest and relevance are fairly obvious, and one which does not assume too much background knowledge, the lack of which can be unnerving to students who are probably somewhat tense in any case. Above all, it is helpful to remember the unconscious learning to which reference has already been made, and to do one's best to ensure that it shall be positive ('this is interesting and I can follow it') rather than negative ('I'm sure it will be too difficult for me'). In the long run, it is of less value for the lecturer to be brilliant and scare the students than for him to be more humdrum if that will reassure them. After all, it is what they learn and not how he performs that matters, and he can defeat his end by too much straining after perfection. It should not be necessary to add that this is not intended as a defence of slipshod preparation, inaccurate material, and boring presentation. But excellence in the lecturer is, by itself, not enough. 'A lecture is not an exercise which has the object of adding to learning – that can be done in books and articles: it is not something to be guarded and modified to meet the possible objections of expert critics who will not be present, or to be made ideally complete to satisfy your own conscience: it is for the service of your audience and you should think of yoursel the whole time as teaching *them*, interesting *them*, and giving *them* what they require and can take' (Clark & Clark, 1959, p. 12).

Written work is often a bugbear to the unpractised adult. It may be tempting to the tutor to gloss over the fact that unwelcome demands will be made; however, as Peers (1958) has insisted, it becomes not easier but harder to introduce the longer it is delayed. If writing is expected, the fact should not be concealed. At the same time, it is common sense to start with tasks that are not too alarming in themselves, either with regard to the difficulty of the subject-matter or with regard to the quantity of work expected. What is feasible will naturally depend on the topic of the course: in many fields of social work, for example, group or individual visits of observation form a popular starting-point, and to prepare simple written reports of these appears both reasonable and acceptable to the students.

Just as preliminary discussions give the tutor a rough sorting of the competent, the merely talkative, and the unforthcoming members of his group, so will early written work give him a certain amount of information about the general level and the individual variations in ability to present material in written form. Again, he knows the point from which he must start and, though it may disappoint him, it is important that he should have this information at an early stage and that he should consider it in relation to the impressions he has already formed from class work. For instance, a sensible and outgoing man of thirty-five, with a mature viewpoint and a wealth of knowledge gained from his experience, may create an excellent first impression in discussion, but be weak in written presentation. If this is not discovered early on, an unduly optimistic picture of the man's capabilities may be formed by the tutor, with subsequent disappointment; also, if written work is going to be part of the basis of later assessment, it is unfair to the individual to be unaware of the situation. At the same time, it is reasonable to expect that such a man has the capacity to improve and that he will respond to instruction and help. Or again, if he were in the sort of class where the tutor lectures all the time and forms his impression of his students' capabilities only from their written work, he might be equally undervalued. It is by considering discussions and written work together that the tutor may form an estimate, not only of the student's present level, but of his potentiality. Obviously, such estimates are still tentative and subject to revision as the student becomes better known.

Speaking generally, it seems fair to say that a tutor without experience of adults, coming perhaps from a research fellowship or from teaching sixth-formers, finds the standard of English lower than he anticipated. At the same time, it is worth while to make a distinction between facility in expression as a technique, and ability to reproduce accurately, think independently, and arrange facts coherently. When all is said and done, it is the latter which is more important. Although they are rarer, one does occasionally come across adults who use facility in English as a means of 'riding away' from serious consideration of issues and it is important they they should not be overvalued.

Written work, then, should involve more than a mere recapitulation of material given in lectures (where a premium is inevitably placed on the possession of a graceful style). The work set at the beginning, though simple in the sense that it does not demand too much background knowledge or too elaborate a scheme of organization, should still demand accuracy, thought, and individual judgement. An account of a visit to a youth club, for instance, will show whether the student can observe, select, and evaluate, even though his sentences may be rather halting, and will give far more useful evidence to his tutor than would a more academic type of essay. Furthermore, by the choice even at this early stage of topics which give scope to the writer if he wishes to add his own comments and opinions, notice is being served on the students that they are expected to think actively about their work and not simply to produce a précis of their lectures or their reading.* This may disconcert some, who supposed that they would be told what to think and do, but it is usually reassuring to most, for adults like to feel that their experience gives them a claim to be heard.

Some tutors, in the initial stages, provide a scheme for students to follow. This ensures that the field is covered without gaps; it is helpful to those who would find it difficult to marshal facts, and is valuable as long as it does not become a bed of Procrustes to which all must conform.

Reading lists are another source of alarm and despondency. Too often a list is simply duplicated and presented to the stu-

* 'We do not help ourselves or others by adding more facts and comments, but by understanding more clearly our problems and theirs' (Richards, 1955, p. 62).

dents without further explanation. The more conscientious ones attempt, with mounting hopelessness, to wade through it; the less conscientious gasp, put it aside, and conveniently forget about it: all alike are learning (in the important unconscious learning to which reference has been made) what it is undesirable for them to learn – that they are inadequate. This is especially the case when courses are grouped, and students in the first few days or evenings attend the lectures of perhaps half a dozen different tutors – and receive as many book lists. Now, granted it is necessary to maintain standards, particularly where the institution concerned is a university or a technical college, but to make the students doubt their capacity is not the best way of achieving this. A useful axiom is that book lists should never be presented to adults who may not have had much academic training without some discussion of their proper use.

In my particular situation I have found it best to have more than one list. A preliminary very short list of simple texts is circulated in advance to the new students (this is only possible, of course, when their names are previously known), giving them an opportunity to fill in serious gaps before the course begins. The majority are usually acquainted with the books on that list; the first impression is consequently one of relief, rather than of inadequacy and dismay. During the initial stages of the course no book list is produced. When the main book list is finally given out, the following points are stressed:

1. Students are not expected to read all the books on the list.
2. Not all the books listed are of equal importance. Certain books will attract some and not others, depending on the individual's special interests and experience.
3. It is important to find one's own level, fulfil one's own particular needs, and go at one's own pace – ignoring the choice, amount, and speed of reading of other students.
4. It is better to read a little and understand it thoroughly

21

than to read a lot without comprehension. What is not really understood will not be assimilated.

5. The list is long for several reasons:

(a) It saves time if particulars of books mentioned in passing in lectures do not have to be taken down by the whole class at dictation speed. Those who are interested can look them up later.

(b) The same topic is treated at different levels of difficulty (examples of this are mentioned).

(c) A wide choice of topics gives scope for different interests. (This can be linked with the multiple lists of grouped courses. Since those attending have varying needs, it is up to them to make their own selection of what will be useful to *them*. Once the basic idea that they are not expected to read everything has been grasped, the rest usually follows.)

6. Lack of time and pressure of other work may prevent one from doing as much reading as one would like, but it can be continued after the course is over; this is not always true of other subjects (e.g. practical work) because of the special facilities needed. It may therefore be sensible to leave some reading until later in order to make the best use of one's time. (The implication here is that a course is not an end in itself but part of a continuing process: this is a thoroughly desirable attitude and indeed it can be said that development after the completion of a course is one test of its value.)

A former student adds: 'I can recall an occasion on which I had a series of examinations to sit on varied subjects. The two papers in which my performance was lowest were those for which I had read most. In these I was tending to reproduce facts, instead of using the facts learned to express an opinion of my own. At the same time, I was not taking advantage of the fact that I had a more mature mind than many of the students who were younger than I. On reflection, I believe I was trying to out-read the younger people and in this way get a good result. My best marks came in the examination connected with morals and ethics, and in these I read much less than in any of the other subjects, but drew upon my own experiences as an adult for help. I am not trying to suggest that one need not read extensively, but one should have a point of view of one's own on which to base reading. Then the adult will never accept blindly all statements in the books, but will question them, and possibly reject them in favour of another view which his own experience suggests is better.'

In sum, book lists are intended to be used flexibly and not as a set of rigid requirements; and students should be left in no doubt that this is so.*

The initial settling-down period can also usefully set the overall standards of tone that are expected of the tutor and of the students. A punctual or unpunctual lecturer will quickly find that he has a punctual or unpunctual class. Once a general mood of slackness and drifting is allowed to set in, it is difficult to eradicate. What is worse, it will tend to spread into the extra-class activities of the group. It may not matter too much if lectures start raggedly, but it matters a good deal if outside commitments and visits are affected by similar slackness. Apart from the discourtesy and thoughtlessness of keeping people waiting, nothing creates more quickly a reputation that the students are indifferent to their work.

Similarly, there is little inducement for students to pause at an untidy noticeboard, flapping with outdated announcements, and it is not surprising if the occasional urgent message is missed. Care of property and equipment, prompt return of library books, satisfactory relations with porters, caretakers, and laboratory assistants, are matters not for precept but for example.

There is no reason why adult students should not act as chairmen at meetings, thus allowing the tutor to take a back

* See, too, the suggestions given in Clark & Clark (1959).

seat and see his group from another viewpoint; in this and many other ways devolution of duties can be encouraged. It is a good plan for the tutor never to do anything that could as well or better be done by somebody else, provided that the devolution is widespread and does not fall on a single hench-man. The particular gifts and knowledge of individuals can be used to full advantage and their energies harnessed to promote the common effort especially if there is reason to suppose that, unharnessed, their energies may be used disruptively. Some obligations must fall on the tutor himself – high among these is the necessity for him to be reasonably available when required. Few things are more aggravating to adults than to be told that their tutor is too busy to see them, particularly if better organization of his time could ease the difficulty, or to be restricted to unduly complicated channels of communication with him.

In these ways, a steady working pattern is built up. No one would wish to make an issue of such matters – indeed, if issues do arise (for instance, the tutor complaining of unpunctuality on visits, or the students feeling aggrieved that they can never see their tutor), they are difficult to resolve and seem a breach of adult dignity. Prevention is better than cure, and the wise tutor attempts to ensure that the social learning of the first days is on lines that he would like to see persist throughout the course.

As the days go by and the group begins to settle down, signs of emerging group feeling can be seen. At first they are rudimentary but later the mixture begins to 'jell'; subgroups form, which may harden into cliques and even into rival factions. A great deal has been written* in recent years on the theory of group formation and the study of sociometry, and it is my intention to deal only with those aspects which are relevant to the work of a tutor of adults. It is more pleasant for

* See, for instance, Mayo (1949), Moreno (1934), Fleming (1949), Sherif & Sherif (1953), Roethlisberger & Dickson (1939), Bion (1961), and Klein (1961).

him, and for everyone else, if intragroup rivalries are kept to a minimum; furthermore, social learning can be an important factor in facilitating or hindering the work of the group. For instance, experienced adults have much that they can teach each other, and the more accessible that expertise is, the better; but it is not going to be accessible if some, or many, are at loggerheads with others. It is, therefore, very much in the interest of the tutor to do what he can to promote pleasant working relationships, not only for their own sake, desirable as they are,* but also for their effects on the knowledge and work of the group. A further, long-term effect applies in certain fields where dealings with people are involved. If, for example, a group of teachers, or of management trainees, practise working smoothly and harmoniously together over a period of time, they are more likely to carry some of this experience back into their actual work than if they had just 'heard of' the theories of Elton Mayo and Lewin, while their actual interpersonal experiences in the group had not been particularly happy. In this way a valuable objective of the course is being realized.

This is not to imply, of course, that no one has had pleasant experiences of working with others before, which would be absurd, but simply that the tutor should do all he can to foster the growth of a friendly spirit and not leave so important a matter to chance. Anyone who has once experienced, as I have, a group that never became a group will realize how much is lost thereby – however delightful the individuals *as* individuals may be. I quote from two written statements from former students, giving contrasting points of view: 'There was no perceptible development of group feeling . . . competitive factors had an adverse effect on such development. . . . Most of us found one more or less congenial figure with whom we have kept in touch but we never really thought of ourselves as a group unless we were united in complaint against a grievance.

* As shown by the famous Hawthorne experiment.

This seems lamentably non-adult when written down, but I believe it to be true of most of us.'

On the other hand: 'Group feeling helps a lot. In the first term I felt very little contact with the group, but individuals impressed me, some for stability and depth, some for friendliness. At the end of the first term the group feeling first started to grow. There were no rivalries on the course, nor factions so far as most of us could see. Everyone liked everyone else and wanted the others to do well. We all had our own subgroups but were all concerned for each other. . . . I think we all found the group feeling helpful. As I read Moreno and Oeser I could see our own course and the truth of much they wrote. . . . A leader can contribute to integration or fragmentation, to unity or disharmony by impartiality or otherwise – it's a factor, possibly critical.'

The emergence of group feeling, however, does not always depend on the tutor: he may do all he can to promote it and still be defeated by circumstances, but at least he will have made an effort. For myself, I would be prepared to take a great deal of trouble to set, in so far as it can be set, a good social climate.

In the first few meetings of a new course, tentative small groups of two or three form (often based on seating, that is, largely on chance); though it is recognized that these fulfil a useful function in countering a feeling of isolation, it is a pity if they persist to become barriers to a wider interplay. Informal activities are helpful in this respect: 'In the large Evening Institute of which I am head, group feeling is fostered by the method of teaching and by the opportunities provided for social contact outside the class. We have found ample evidence of this during this session. I opened a canteen providing only tea and biscuits, and instituted a ten-minute break so that students could attend the canteen. This has been highly successful and one can feel the difference it has made within the Centre – it has come alive. We find that group feeling can be fostered within the smaller group of the class if the students are given some opportunity to talk together. This is done in some classes, such as cookery, embroidery, needlework, etc., while the work is in progress. In other classes we have a break from work in order to give them an opportunity to have completely informal talk (rather like children in the playground)' (F.S.).

Preliminary discussions can be valuable, as I have suggested, in helping people to get to know one another, and the tutor should make frequent use of students' names. Often, the more forthcoming members can be asked to make a short statement on some aspect of their experience which may be of general interest and on which they can be questioned afterwards. It is important here not to suggest that solo performances are being given, nor to set the speakers up as individual 'experts', since this might result in barring them off from the rest of the group; but rather to focus attention on the needs of the group which are being met from within its own ranks. In the first case the effect is subtly divisive, whereas it is cohesion that should be stressed above all else. In the second case it is implied that Mr. A. has helped the group on this occasion and that the other members too have knowledge and experience which it is hoped they will be equally ready to put into the pool and from which all can benefit.

This attitude is the antithesis of the notion that there is a copyright in ideas. It is sometimes suggested that teachers in particular have been possessive in the past, owing to a theory that it is 'wrong' to copy, but that this possessiveness and secretiveness are gradually decreasing and that an attitude of cooperation and more open acknowledgement of the help of others is replacing the old individualist outlook. Whether or not this is so, willingness to give and to accept can be a valuable aid in developing group feeling. 'When each person feels that his own opinions can be put forward and will be given serious consideration by the rest of the group, then the feeling of belonging to the group will grow' (F.S.).

Visits of observation are particularly useful, too, especially if they are organized so that numbers are kept small, and so that the same people do not always join the same parties. Some intervention from the tutor may be necessary here, to prevent undue crystallization into sets; for just as visits provide opportunities for friendly informal social mixing, they offer also a temptation to students always to go with their friends and thereby miss the value of wider contacts. Adults will see the reasonableness of an extended variety of companions from the point of view of work, but a most valuable by-product is the ease of understanding that is promoted throughout the group and not only among a few. A test of successful policy in this respect is seen later in the course, when members suddenly realize that they sign up for a visit purely in terms of its probable value to them and without reflecting first who else is going and whether they will be welcome, because they can take this for granted.

A tutor who wishes to set a friendly tone also needs to consider seriously his own jokes and asides and make sure that these do not set up gratuitous competition. For instance, a hostel warden with a degree in mathematics is unwise to indulge too freely in the sort of pleasantries that egg on the mathematics students at the expense of the others. Again, an ageing partisan of Cambridge cannot forget his attitudes of forty years ago, and though this may seem a harmless and even amusing foible its implications are less so. North versus south, men versus women, technical versus grammar – the possibilities of stirring up dissension are endless if one wants an easy laugh. It is done quickly and almost unconsciously by the kind of person who likes taking sides, but such immaturity, even though it may pass – just – with young students, is entirely out of place where adults are concerned. One's aim is to smooth down rivalries, not stir them up: there are probably enough existing sources of tension without adding to them unnecessarily.

Inescapable competitiveness – as distinct from the manufactured sort – is a more serious problem. The effect of keenness in a group, extremely interested and with high group morale, is to increase productiveness and to raise standards of work (in fact, often the group is the firmest and safest guardian of its own standard). A point may be reached, however, where the high expectations set by the group become immoderate. The greatest danger of overpressure comes not from outside authority – the requirements of the syllabus or the urgings of the tutor – but from trying to keep up with one's peers. Most adult students are conscientious and responsible and if they are not quite sure what is expected of them, or what the standard is, they are very vulnerable to competition from each other. This competition may be intensified if marks of merit, for instance distinctions, are attainable. (Having worked with such a system for ten years, I am not myself in favour of distinctions, and would prefer that students should simply pass or fail, but nevertheless this is a side issue.) The main pressure comes not from the quest for glory, which is probably confined to a few, but from the uncertainties of the many. I shall have more to say about the effect of uncertainty in Chapter 6, but the point at issue here is the strength of group pressure. It is the tutor's responsibility to keep an eye on the development of group feeling and, though he may welcome keenness as a sign of good morale, to make sure that it does not become over-pressure, particularly on the weaker members of the group. A frantic attempt to 'keep up with the Joneses' tends to be self-perpetuating once it has started, and the best way to combat it is to emphasize and re-emphasize the fact of individual differences, and that expectations and goals necessarily vary from person to person. It is for the student to appraise his needs realistically and set his sights accordingly – only in this way will the tyranny of group pressure, which is the obverse of strong group feeling, be avoided. It is a problem to which there is no easy answer, but certainly one of which the tutor should be aware.*

* A full discussion and analysis of morale can be found in Leighton (1946).

Finally, there is the problem of the awkward individual, who begins to stand out as the group settles down.

'Social relationships within the student body may cause irritation and individual problems to arise which are not always helpful either to the individual or to the group. I think it is fair to say that the majority of adult students work together as a well-knit social group, out to help each other and gain the knowledge and qualifications which they are all seeking, but it is quite disturbing to come across the exceptions to these circumstances, such as the student who, having completed an excellent piece of work, tries to hide it away and not discuss it with his colleagues, as he feels it may help them too much and they may begin to vie with him in his position as the bright boy of the group. Childish, we know, but it does happen on occasions even with adults.

'Then there is the student who, having listened to some of the more vociferous of his colleagues exhibiting their knowledge of the subject under study, gets a feeling of inferiority and is almost terrified to open his mouth during discussions in case he is rather off the beam and may be ridiculed for what he feels is his lack of knowledge.

'Even amongst adults one occasionally finds the individual who sets himself up to become "teacher's pet" in the hope of making a good impression, presumably because he erroneously feels that if his work is not quite up to standard he may be allowed to scrape through, or because he hopes that he may gain some distinctive report' (F.S.).

Broadly speaking, these awkward individuals can be divided into two groups, isolates and disruptors. People have a right to be solitary if they so wish, and there is no case for badgering or even jollying along those who are more reserved than the rest, provided that they are happy in their isolation; at the same time, failure to fit in with the group can be damaging to the confidence of the individual (alternatively, it may already have been damaged), and the part of the tutor in this case is unobtrusive encouragement. Aggressive individuals can be a source of real anxiety to the tutor, not least because they threaten his security as well as the harmony of the group; and so I have dealt with them in some detail in the later chapters of this book. Here I shall say only that the important determinant is whether they care about their work or not. The great majority of adults (even the difficult ones) do care, and the tutor can be encouraged by that fact for the trials ahead. It has also to be recognized bluntly that no tutor has any hold on those who genuinely (and not just as a matter of bravado) have little interest in their work. What we have to avoid doing is turning the former into the latter by our own ineptitude.

In most cases, however, membership of a friendly group with common interests can be a very rewarding and stimulating experience. I believe that what I have called 'social learning' is very important and, therefore, I have dealt with it at length before turning now to consider the more obvious ingredients of instruction and learning.

Chapter Three

LECTURING

IT IS ODD that comparatively little has been written about lecturing when one considers how continual is its practice (or mispractice). If the assumption is that we all possess the skill fully developed on the day that we sign our contract and are therefore not in need of critical examination or improvement, it is blatantly false. There may be a few natural lecturers, but there are many more, such as myself, whose progress is a long, faltering search, and others who have given up searching. It is worth considering what part lecturing plays as a means of instruction of adult students.

Brilliant lecturers can be dealt with quickly. There are always a few outstanding figures whom it is unquestionably profitable for students of any age to hear, even if only once, as an occasion to remember. 'Yes, I heard Sir John Jones, it must be twenty years ago. I was tremendously impressed by him, not so much by what he said (I'm a bit hazy about that now), but by the stamp of quality. One felt the distinction of his mind and caught the excitement of his discoveries.' Evidently Sir John 'spoke with authority and not as one of the scribes'.

Such figures are rare. Rather more common is the man who, though not of outstanding distinction of mind, has an unusual gift of lucid and compelling presentation and can 'put over his stuff' (note the revealing phrase) in such a way as to rouse the enthusiastic interest of his hearers. It is this man who is usually thought of as 'a brilliant lecturer', and so he is rightly in great demand on special occasions and his regular lecture courses are extremely popular. Bruce Truscot (1943) has considered the contribution of this type of lecturer in detail and his general conclusion is that, as far as the young undergraduates of whom he is speaking are concerned, it is of some value: the test of that value is to be found in how far the 'inspirational' lecture does actually inspire the students and how far the enthusiastic interest aroused is followed out in increased diligence thereafter. Much of this applies also, I would say, to older students, but to a less degree than to the younger: adults are less likely to be carried away by a polished performance (some of them may indeed be unfairly suspicious of it); in that case, the subjective value being less to them, everything will depend on the objective value of the lecture – its solid stuff as well as its attractive surface.

However, men of international reputation, and naturally brilliant lecturers, are both uncommon. These aside, let us turn to the more ordinary situation where a reasonably competent tutor faces an adult group, because I believe that the traditional lecture pattern is open to considerable criticism in such a setting.

The set lecture has been the usual mode of instruction for many centuries in the universities. Even there, with a pre-dominantly undergraduate audience, it has attracted dubious comment as anachronistic.* Outside the universities and with older students, these doubts are increased. Consider the follow-ing points:

1. The obvious criticism that too much emphasis is placed on oral communication and too little use is made of modern visual and other aids applies more strongly when the group is a non-academic one.
2. A certain homogeneity in background information may perhaps be assumed in an undergraduate class in, say,

* See Truscot (1943) and Moberley (1949).

33

physics, but the range of previous knowledge and experience in many adult classes is usually wider.

3. The danger of unreal and insincere learning.

Of these, the third point seems to me the most important and I should like to develop it in full, making it clear that I am considering not only the posing lecturer but also the posing audience: in fact, of the two the latter is the more likely.

The insincere lecturer can be dealt with quickly. He deals in frothy generalities that sound good but do not stand up to serious consideration: consequently, he rarely has serious influence. A lecturer, however, can be perfectly sincere and yet fail to connect with his audience. What he is saying may be too difficult or too uninterestingly presented, but in either case his hearers are not really taking in what he is saying – though they may be, and probably are, taking it down. I am not thinking here of the extreme case where signs of boredom are obvious, but of the more usual situation where the lecturer is trying and the audience are trying, but there is a gap between. They are adults and can simulate an attentive air,* and the ordinarily sensitive lecturer has no means of knowing that he is meeting a façade. One of two things then happens, as far as his hearers are concerned: the more hopeful is that they drop their masks when alone with each other ('I didn't understand that.' 'Neither did I'); the worse alternative is that they retain the masks and tell themselves as well as each other that they understand perfectly. To keep up this pose is hard work, and unprofitable; it is far more serious to deceive oneself than to deceive others, and anyone who cannot admit to himself that he is out of his depth is indeed in a bad way.

Another way of putting this is to say that certain students expect to be fogged and tend rather to despise what is clear and simple. They become used to a blurred focus and in the end

---

* As one of my former students put it, 'Adults can sleep with their eyes open even better than children!'

hardly notice that it is blurred. As well as the fog that is produced by woolly and orotund language, blurring can result from the academic habit of calling in clouds of witnesses to testify to every point, however banal. We are all familiar with this type of thing – the lecture is a summary of previous research on the chosen topic, or of American novelists of the last fifty years, or of Great Discoverers – whatever the ostensible subject,* it rapidly becomes a list of names. The work of Binks, Winks, Spinks, Przemysl, and many others is rapidly pigeon-holed and the students' pens fly. What a lot of ground is being covered! Never mind if some of it is incorrectly copied, so that the work of Winks is attributed to Binks; and even if Przemysl is omitted altogether (although he is the most important) as being too difficult to spell, there will still be plenty to learn by heart afterwards.†

The results of an academic diet of this kind are:

1. What is valuable is lost among the trivial; nothing stands out.‡
2. Topics are treated out of proportion to their importance, depending on how much 'research' can be cited.
3. The often conflicting viewpoints are left unresolved.
4. Students tend to lose sight of the wood for the trees.

It is irresistible to quote here I. A. Richards's brilliant gloss in *Speculative Instruments* (1955, p. 101) on the Babes in the Wood as over-zealous scholars: 'They went every-

---

* I have tried to take examples that might come up in different fields of adult work – thus the first might come in an academic evening course at a university, the second in a Workers' Educational Association class, the third in popular science at a technical college.

† 'The pursuit of knowledge in order merely to satisfy the examiner is a process which can hardly go very deep' (Armfelt, *Education: New Hopes & Old Habits*, 1949, p. 54).

‡ Sir Charles Morris said in his Foreword to *Trends in English Adult Education* (Raybould (Ed.), 1959): 'There can be little doubt in my view that in all parts of education from the grammar school upwards every student is nowadays trying to acquire and hold knowledge of far more detail than he can handle. I would add that detail which is beyond one's capacity to handle not only is wasted but harmfully and progressively clutters up the workshop of the mind.'

where but out of the wood and were found in the morning . . . under a heap of leaves. The story says that pitying
birds buried them so. This seems a pretty fancy. I find it
more likely that they collected those leaves themselves and
perished through unregulated interest in the variety of
foliation.'
5. Instead of thinking for themselves, students work at
second-hand. Reading takes the place of experience, and
written work becomes a hotch-potch of other people's
writing.

I do not intend to suggest that armchair 'thinking' is a
substitute for facts: quite the reverse. But I do suggest that
the opposite tendency, to consider that the painstaking
collecting of facts is a substitute for thinking and feeling, is
to be deplored. Nothing can take the place of an honest
attempt to work things out for oneself, at one's own level,
low though that may be; and to subsume whatever factual
knowledge one possesses – and the wider the better – in an
orderly framework. Only so can one's knowledge be made
one's own.

Conventional higher education tends only too often to be
second-hand and second-rate: as Whitehead (1955, p. 79) put
it trenchantly, 'The second-handedness of the learned world is
the secret of its mediocrity'. The same point has been made
more fully by Moberley and Truscot, and I shall leave them to
describe the effects as far as the young undergraduate is concerned. My concern is with older people and I think it is fair to
summarize their reactions as follows:

1. They know that they are rather rusty as compared with
younger people.
2. They want to do the right thing – 'Tell us what is expected and we'll have a go'.
3. They may or may not have acquired a stereotype as to
what *is* expected. If they have, and it is an unfortunate one,

it may be difficult to dispel; on the other hand, it is often a relief to a non-academic adult to discover that he need not be something other than he is.

4. They may be more impatient of sham learning than younger students, provided their stereotype does not stand in the way – that is, provided they can recognize it as sham. If not, they may be more gullible.

5. A fresh perception can be both easier and harder for older men and women to attain – easier because they are less used to being directed, harder because their prejudices have had longer to get entrenched and because of their lack of training in recognizing fallacious modes of reasoning. This could be summed up as saying that they are less used to being told *what* to think and feel, but they are also less used to being told *how* to think.

6. Older people have a fund of knowledge from their own experience against which the claims of theories can be tested. They are not all prepared to trust their experience, nor is it all valuable, but on the whole their pooled knowledge stretches over a wide area.

7. Following on from this, the balance of first-hand and second-hand knowledge differs in older and younger students. In the case of older people, their first-hand knowledge may be deeper, but narrow, and their greatest need is to relate what they have experienced to a wider context. To some extent, this wider context can be provided by the experiences of others, or by theory. The worst thing is if no relation is made between what they learn now and their previous experience. Cross-fertilization between the present and the past is essential.

8. The attitude of older people to their work is more serious than that of young students: they have more at stake. 'Polite' tolerance of boredom is less likely: if they do not like what they are given, they may protest or cease to come, but they will not stay and waste their time.

It seems, therefore, that the needs of older students demand above all an approach based on their first-hand experience – which uses it, sifts it, relates it to a corpus of knowledge, and in so doing enriches it. Realism is then the prime virtue; unreality and remoteness (which so quickly lead to insincerity) are the worst failing. 'Only connect', said Forster in *Howard's End*, and this might well be the motto of those who have to teach older people.

At this stage a critic may feel: 'That is all very well, but it is true of all teaching, not merely of teaching adults. It is obvious that we have to start where the learner is – what I want to know is how to find out where he is. It is obvious that learning should be an active process – what I want to know is how to make it so.' It can be readily agreed that the principle holds throughout but, obvious as it may be, it is worth stating explicitly because it is so often ignored. How to put it into practice is, of course, the heart of the matter, to which I now turn.

'Active learning' is a phrase that is much used at the present time, and also much misused. The intention is to contrast the passivity of absorption (a sponge holding water) with the active process of adjustment involved in learning ('putting in' with 'drawing out of'). As far as children are concerned, the usual contrast is between 'learning by rote' and 'learning by doing': so far, so good. Unfortunately, 'activity' tends to be thought of exclusively in terms of bodily movement, and not in its wider meaning of activity of mind. (It was a wise headmaster who said 'I interpret "activity" as "activity of mind".') As children grow older, they are less dependent on concrete expression, and so 'activity' (as expressed in bodily movement) is less evident, but it is a sad day if 'active learning' in its wider sense ceases.* So with older children and with adults there is every reason to retain the phrase 'active learning', and to apply it to those situations where the learner's interest is fully caught and where

* Cf. Whitehead (1955, p. 58), 'An education which does not begin by evoking initiative and end by encouraging it must be wrong.'

he is concentrating his whole mind and body on what he is doing, irrespective of whether it is woodwork, music, a geometrical theorem, or a problem of philosophy (in order of increasing abstractness) that occupies him so intently.

The distinction between concrete and abstract is by no means the same as that between active learning and its opposite, and should not be confused with it. The important thing is the genuine concern that the learner has for his work: he is active when he is thinking intently though motionless, and equally, he is *not* actively learning when he is merely banging things together or mouthing a page of print, with his mind far away, though in the one case his hands and in the other his vocal organs are busy. I would prefer, therefore, to interpret 'active learning' along the lines of genuine concern, of sincere concentration, and leave aside as red herrings the physical and concrete characteristics of the task. How far those characteristics may *facilitate* learning is, of course, another matter.

Our question then becomes, how can we make learning an active process, and how can we find out 'where the learners are' since that will give us our starting-point. Put in those terms, the question answers itself: the simplest way is by letting them tell us, and for that we have to look and listen. The more we do ourselves (whether by way of exposition, demonstration, or lecture – depending on the nature of the subject involved), the less chance we are giving our students of showing us 'where they are'. Yet this is the knowledge we most need, in order to make our instruction genuinely meaningful to them. If we do not give them the opportunity to show us directly, we must perforce rely on indirect methods of estimating interest and attention – as, for instance, if they *appear* to be attending (yet it has already been said that this can be simulated). What is more, even if they are interested, if they are making a genuine attempt to follow the tutor's argument or demonstration, it is still not certain that they are doing so successfully. There may be gaps in their knowledge of which neither he nor they are aware, and which will prevent the whole thing from clicking into place.

'What nonsense!', says the critic, 'of course I can find out whether they have taken in what I have told them or demonstrated to them. I can get them to reproduce my actions or I can set them examination questions at the end of the course, and then I will know whether they are clear as between Binks and Winks.' The difficulty there is that it is knowledge *post factum*, and comes when it is too late to make any difference: the unfortunate students have already failed, the stable door is locked after the horse has gone. A university lecturer recently said: 'I had a most unpleasant shock this week when I marked the Finals papers. One candidate is quite hopeless. Yet he has done essays regularly for two years and they always seemed respectable enough: I think he must have got by by copying chunks out of books.' It is quite evident that there were gaps in the tutor's knowledge of that student, and gaps also between the student's apparent competence and his real comprehension. Now granted that this is an example from a different field and that a university department may reasonably hope to assume the competence of its candidates, yet education too often proceeds as if its task were to pour knowledge into a recipient, whereas the establishment of meaningful connections is the primary task. It is easy to pay lip-service to the latter as a principle, but when it comes to the point in practice many lecturers cover the syllabus and hope for the best. So do the students: and hence that disturbing phenomenon, the students who do *not* fail, who produce not only respectable essays but also respectable regurgitations of these in Finals, and yet do not really connect their work with anything outside it. It all remains external and somehow ineffective. In contrast, when the tutor knows his students and their difficulties, and the students understand what they are doing and why they are doing it, then there is a chance that the syllabus will be not only 'covered', but learned *effectively*.

The basic disadvantage, then, of the 'set' lecture is that it is a one-way process. However competent it is of its kind, it may go for nothing for one or more students because it does not connect adequately with anything in their experience. The flow of knowledge is like a tap which is turned on, and the students' minds (or notebooks) are buckets which may or may not be in position to be filled.

In contradistinction to this is what I propose to call the teaching lecture, whose chief characteristic is that it involves considerable interplay between the tutor and the group that he is teaching. The tutor takes some responsibility that his students should *learn* as a result of their time with him – he does not cast his pearls and leave it to chance whether or not they are picked up. In case this sounds unduly like spoon-feeding, I hasten to add that the final responsibility for learning is and must remain with the student, but the tutor has the responsibility of seeing that he on his side has done all he can to make it a meaningful process. On the contrary, it is the 'set' lecturer, who doles out gobbets of predigested material which he expects his students to swallow without chewing, who is doing the spoon-feeding.

In a teaching lecture the tutor does his best to choose examples which will be meaningful to *that particular* audience. If he knows that a number of them have visited a certain hospital or institution, he will take that rather than another as his example, and he will call where possible on the relevant experience of members of the group for other examples. Their statements may be framed less concisely than his would have been and may not bring out the vital point; but this is a risk that the tutor can gladly take, remembering that the gain in concreteness to his group is worth more than a few seconds lost, and he can always clinch the point himself if he feels that the speaker did not do so. 'You mean that the National Health Service now . . .' (followed by a re-statement of the example to bring out the point) can quickly provide the context. If the tutor had given the example himself, no doubt it would have been in its context in the first place, but who is to say whether it would have been rightly placed *in the wider context of the student's experience?*

While he is speaking, the tutor watches the faces of his audience and is alert for momentary hesitations or gleams of insight. The quick addition of a synonym alongside an unknown word may be sufficient help, or a question (such as 'Would you like me to say that again?' or 'Haven't I made it clear, Mr. Smith?') can make it easy for lack of understanding to be avowed. 'Can you tell us how that has worked in your experience, Miss Evans?' enlists support from the gleam in the eye. 'You look as if you've all had a tiring day' may be stating no more than the truth, but to say it at all suggests a warmth and humanity in the lecturer, an absence of remoteness, a willingness to make allowances for flagging vitality and attention, and, above all, a readiness to realize that adults are not just learning machines but have other preoccupations and worries which they cannot entirely slough off by merely entering the doors of an Evening Institute. If the tutor realizes that many of his audience are tired, he will not unduly blame himself for their yawns – but the glassy eye, the blank expression, and the doodling hand can all in other circumstances give a salutary jerk to his complacency. It should not be possible, during a meeting of adults, for a sizeable section of an audience of thirty to engage consistently (though quietly) in activities unrelated to the purpose of the meeting, but I have known it happen where the principal speaker is insensitive to his audience and watches his notes rather than their faces. 'There is a book, who runs may read' does not refer to printed matter, as the tutor might well remember.

Question-time comes traditionally at the end of the lecture hour, but there is a great deal to be said for allowing (I would say, encouraging) questions at any time. Mistakes and misunderstandings can be cleared up on the spot before they have had time to become entrenched. Some questions sound silly in isolation half an hour later and their true purport is not realized, others are forgotten altogether, and the net result is an impoverishment of understanding. It is not my experience that the right to interrupt is misused, and, even if it is, the remedy is in the hands of the tutor, backed by public opinion. Occasionally, one or two students (usually of the more 'educated' type, who have been well drilled themselves in sitting mum) have been impatient of others' queries, which they regard as breaking the thread, but the majority greatly prefer the possibility of elucidating what puzzles them immediately – and so should the tutor if he really wishes to forward understanding and not parrot acceptance. I doubt whether this method takes up much additional time, because questions at the end often need supplementaries before the lecturer can be sure he is on to the right matter, so that more time is spent on each one, though there may be fewer of them. In any case, it is time well spent, for the lecturer who scamps on understanding has not saved much. Less work done thoroughly is better than more done without comprehension. Peers (1958, p. 228) has justifiably criticized the pseudo-discussion that sometimes follows a set lecture, when each question is the signal for a further ten-minute discourse by the lecturer, and interaction among the group is at a minimum. Questions on the spot would curb this type of verbose lecturer, for at least he would realize that it was his own time he was wasting.

The matter of interruptions other than questions is more debatable. So far, it may be said, the lecturer is keeping control in his own hands: he can choose whether or not to ask for examples and who shall supply them, and the apparent freedom to interrupt with questions is at least limited by their linkage to what he has said; whereas a general liberty to interrupt might appear to risk licence. Perhaps this is as far as a tutor who is not very sure of his group should go, and one who is haunted by the fear of a chaotic free-for-all, in which the

43

thread of his lecture is completely broken, would perhaps be wiser to be cautious until he knows his students better.

Nevertheless, there is much value, if a tutor has confidence that he can do so and still retain the initiative, in welcoming interruptions other than direct questions. Such contributions may amplify a point, or call attention to a supporting line of argument, or throw doubt on the validity of what has been said. An insecure tutor is not likely to relish any of these possibilities; his dislike for them will be proportionate to their ascending order of enormity. If he resents even amplification as a denial of his omniscience, he is less likely still to put up with a direct challenge to his authority, however politely and reasonably it may be phrased. Yet if the benefit of the group, and not his self-esteem, is the deciding factor, there is much to be said for contributions of all these kinds. Take the most controversial, the last. It is highly probable that the tutor is right in his contention, but if there is doubt it should be ventilated. A simple misapprehension on the student's part is better cleared up at once. Perhaps it has been aided because the tutor's language was less than crystal clear – if so, it is probably shared by several others and should be instantly corrected. Denial of an immediate outlet does not prevent criticism later, with the additional barb, 'He didn't seem all that sure of it when he shut you up so quickly'. Milton's famous words in *Areopagitica* can profitably be recollected here: 'Let Truth and falsehood grapple; who ever knew Truth put to the worse in a free and open encounter?'

But supposing the student is in fact right? To be caught out in an inaccuracy is a nightmare of the insecure tutor, for how (he fears) will his students respect him if he patently does not know? In fact, however, an honest admission of error or at least of uncertainty will gain more respect than an attempt to botch it over. I can remember on my very first day of lecturing as an adult tutor shying at an inconvenient question, and hedging. I knew that I had hedged and so, too, no doubt, did everyone else; and though they might condone it in the circumstances, the underlying insecurity was more patent than an admission of ignorance. It is worth asking ourselves whether the pose of omniscience justifies the risk, and whether it is not simpler in the long run to be frank about our limitations and to be ready to say 'I don't know'.

So far, it is suggested that it is the insecure lecturer who clamps down on interruptions; though this is sometimes the case, there are often other perfectly valid considerations of time and relevance for limiting them. It is the tutor's responsibility to see that the time is used to the best advantage, that the thread is clear to follow, and that the greatest good of the greatest number is considered. (More of this will be said in the next chapter, on Discussion.) It *may* be the best use of the time to consolidate understanding by traversing and re-traversing the same ground, rather than try to cover all that the lecturer had initially hoped; but if on some occasion he thinks that this is not the wisest plan, he cannot shirk his duty to guide by putting the onus on the group – 'If this is what they want to do, then let them'.

From all that has been said, it follows that a teaching lecture differs from a set lecture in being unrepeatable. A set lecture takes no particular account of its audience and so, once it has been prepared, it can be repeated (apart from revision to bring its material up to date) over several years. There is the apocryphal story of the lecturer who delivered his wonted course of lectures just as before, keeping it up for the whole session, in spite of having that year an audience of only one. There are other stories of books that cannot be published until their authors retire, otherwise they would have no material for their lectures. Whatever the truth of these anecdotes, they have in common the suggestion that the audience is a negligible factor, a constant, and it is this suggestion that I wish to controvert.*
A teaching lecture demands as much accuracy and care in its preparation as a set lecture, but having given it that careful

* One adult tutor destroys his notes after lecturing, so that he will not be tempted to use them again as they stand.

preparation, the tutor of adults should be willing to let some of his lecture go if the needs of the particular situation demand it. His work is contingent, and has reference to what *may* happen and what *this* group requires; it does not exist unalterable, like Platonic Ideas, in what is only too likely to be a vacuum. The tutor gains in flexibility and in effectiveness, but the demands on him are greater: they are demands that he should teach and not merely lecture.

It would be a tempting generalization to say that the skill used in imparting knowledge often varies inversely with the difficulty of the subject-matter. The teacher of young children, or of backward ones, cannot afford to neglect the mechanics of learning; the teacher of older, brighter pupils can sometimes hope that the children will learn, in spite of the limitations of his presentation – and, unfortunately, grammar-school, training-college, and university methods sometimes leave much to be desired. Teachers in these places get by because of the ability of their pupils and their own prestige, but their *methods* are sometimes more primitive than those that the infant school or the 'C' stream in the secondary modern school could afford for long.* I am not advocating apparatus where it is not necessary, but I believe that no system that abstracts from the characteristics of the learners can do so without loss of depth and soundness – without becoming 'instruction' rather than 'education'.

The unfortunate thing is that the prestige held by advanced studies tends to be radiated as a nimbus, even when the halo is not particularly deserved. It used to be argued, for instance, that Latin trained the mind, when it was the ability of the Latin students that made them successful, not their Latin work; and similarly there is a halo round the academic lecture, because it is associated with able minds in a university, which it hardly merits in its own right. It is arguable that these able minds

---

* A physicist who watched a demonstration of teaching a handicapped child – technically a brilliant performance – completely missed seeing the skill involved, because the content of the lesson was so small and the pace so slow by his standards.

might progress even further with *better* methods of teaching (and certainly the existence of bored, apathetic, and discouraged grammar-school and university alumni is not easy to justify), but this argument need not be pursued here. My present purpose is to call attention to the drawbacks of set lectures as far as adult students are concerned, while admitting that they are easier for a beginning tutor, or one who is not sure of his material, to prepare. It would be a great pity if the weaknesses of academic instruction were copied in, for instance, tutorial classes and university diploma courses, on the grounds of 'providing higher education' and 'raising standards'. Standards must be set, and maintained, but the best way of achieving this is to see that the goals set for the class are reasonable and that the methods chosen to attain them are realistic – otherwise it is all so much moonshine.

In summary, the case against set lectures for adult students rests on two simple facts – adults have limitations and they have assets – both of which must be taken into account. Compared with the average young full-time students in college or university, adults generally have gaps in their background knowledge and a greater range in attainment, so that a set lecture 'misses the boat' very frequently. On the other hand, they can often contribute much of value from their personal experience, and a system which neglected to tap this rich source would indeed be foolish. 'Adults bring experience and can contribute. Tutors must accept this. They also bring prejudices which they may want to air (air is a good sweetener and even prejudices may have some basis of rightness)' (F.S.).

I believe that the success of a class for adults is proportionate to its ability to harness and use the contributions of its members. Not merely is there a psychological value for the individual in feeling that he has something to add to the common sum, which is helpful in giving confidence to go forward, but in so doing he is necessarily relating his own piece of the jigsaw to the whole and so what he learns will have point and meaning.

47

Chapter Four

DISCUSSION

HERE IS an example. The discussion has been going for about ten minutes and is just beginning to liven up, but it is still pretty fluid and may or may not develop usefully. Key sentences only of each contribution are given. The topic is juvenile delinquency.

   A But we've all done things like that ourselves, surely? I know I have. (*Murmurs of assent.*)

It seems as if they will take this further, but the next contribution starts a new line.

   B So far everybody has talked as if only boys were delinquent. But I think the girl delinquent is a more serious problem.
   C Oh no, it's three times as common among boys.

She has got her facts wrong, but her point is clear. However, it isn't B's point.

   B I didn't mean that.
   D I agree with B. There may be fewer girls in the courts, but a really difficult girl is harder to deal with than a difficult boy. I remember . . .

(*Further anecdotes follow on the same theme.*) It appears as if the question of sex differences in delinquency is going to be considered, but E returns to A's point.

E I remember being chased by the farmer when . . .

It is evident that his mind has continued to consider the original lead. The introduction of anecdotes, though on a different point, has emboldened him to bring out one of his own. The association of ideas is not logical, but often happens. This is the first time that E has ever joined in a discussion and he makes no further intervention this morning. The tutor may be pardoned for feeling disappointed that a sequence which promised to develop has been wrenched astray (and in a rather banal fashion), but is glad to see that E has gathered confidence to join in. Which way will it go now?

A That is what I say. Why should they be stigmatized as delinquent when they are no worse than we are?

A is glad to have the chance of returning to his point. His generalization, however, is rather sweeping. An argument follows, which has the effect of correcting A.

D We seem to be arguing rather about words. Would it help if we said what we mean?
F We all mean different things. (*Laughter.*)
D No, but some of us talk about doing things which are against the law, and others put the emphasis on having got caught.

D's points are sound (it will be remembered that implicit in his previous remark was a useful distinction between the frequency of female offenders and the difficulty of reclaiming them), but unfortunately his manner is rather aggressive and he puts the

49

others off. The leader notices that he is both able and contentious. It seems worth intervening at this point, to prevent the value of D's suggestion being lost.

> TUTOR You mean that we should stick to those that are brought into court?
>
> D Yes.
> G Yes, as long as we remember that there is a fair amount of hidden delinquency, like an iceberg. Also, it is a moral question as well as an administrative one.

The door is now closed on personal reminiscence, the tutor hopes. It is unlikely that anyone present has a court record.

> T That's a good point. It rather sounds from what you say that you would cut out from our discussion offences that are purely technical?

He hopes to forestall a digression on riding without lights.

> G Yes, I'd rather talk about what it is in the person himself that leads him into difficulties.

This is a new issue and promises well. G is influential and popular.

> H Or his surroundings.
> I I think we can overdo the surroundings business. There are plenty of children in my evening club whose circumstances are appalling, but none of them has been in court.

(*Several elaborate this.*) In the course of this, many of the factors that are often found in association with delinquency are mentioned.

> C Burt says. . . . (*she proceeds to cite Sir Cyril Burt.*)
> G It seems strange that some children will pass unaffected through difficulties that are sufficient to sink others.

D I think what G has said is extremely important. Perhaps we could talk about it a bit. I read somewhere – I think it was Mannheim* – that the biggest puzzle in delinquency is immunity.

B What did you say that book was called? (D *gives it.*)
H How do you spell it?
D It's on the book list.

The interchange here between D and the others is more favourable. D's attitude to G's suggestion is positive, and B and H show signs of readiness to follow his lead. Again what D says is thoughtful.

B It rather suggests that it is no good landing on one thing and saying 'this is *the* reason' because there are so many exceptions either way.

The group then settle down and discuss why some children are not delinquent in spite of unfavourable conditions. About ten join in. The major contributions come from B, D, and G. Eventually . . .

G It comes back in the end to the individual.
J Will-power.

This seems rather naïve, but one sees what she means. J continues more firmly:

J If you've got enough determination you can overcome anything.

(*Much dissent and doubt expressed.*) Most realize that what J has said does not advance the matter. Their criticisms are temperate

* Carr-Saunders, Mannheim & Rhodes (1942), *Young Offenders.*

but J is not allowed to get away with it. The tutor attempts a rescue.

> T We seem always to return to the interaction between 'what sort of person this is' and 'what is happening around him'. If he had a bit of help, perhaps he could –
> D (*interrupting*) – decide to go straight and really pull it off, if only others helped at the critical moment. I don't believe that anybody is really beyond helping – at least he may be hopeless now, but he might not have been once.

What he says is not very clearly expressed, but interjections and suggestions from the others make him clarify his position, which is a denial that anybody is ever 'born irretrievably bad'. This is a promising lead, and the new topic continues for the remainder of the time. It ends in a hubbub, with D overreaching himself once more and arousing opposition, and several talking at once. Of the twenty-five present, about six have been silent throughout, and three or four others have joined in only to assent or dissent from time to time, but they look as if they have been following with interest. The remainder have been actively concerned, and although D and a few others were particularly prominent they by no means monopolized the proceedings. At the end, K and L, who have not spoken, come up to the tutor with a question based on a point raised earlier which they have evidently discussed quietly together. As the group breaks up to go to the canteen, fragments of about eight conversations are to be heard. Some are about the Test match but others (not less animated) pick up again one or other of the questions discussed earlier. (*Exeunt omnes, arguing.*)

Now evidently there has been interest and enjoyment, but the question is how far the time has been profitable. The flaws in the proceedings are fairly obvious, but the only reasonable comparison is not with an ideal never likely to be realized, but with the ordinary common-or-garden lecture situation, given a lecturer and an audience who are all less than archangels.

The great advantage of the discussion situation, it seems to me, is in a certain earthiness and realism and absence of pretension. Whatever its failings, and they are many, the average run-of-the-mill discussion at least mirrors only too truly the limitations of its participants. It may seem odd to hold this as a virtue, but the result is that it catches people where they are. I do not claim that insincere posing, of the kind deprecated in the last chapter, is impossible in a discussion situation, but only that it is vastly more difficult than in a lecture situation both for it to occur and for it to be undetected. It is worth considering how the discussion quoted, and others like it,* could help a tutor to know his students' strong and weak points, as against, for example, the lecturer in the previous chapter who, judging from essays alone, knew of serious weaknesses only when it was too late.

It is immediately evident that the weaknesses stand out much more clearly in the discussion – for instance, A's too-sweeping generalization, J's readiness to apply labels and consider that sufficient, the shifting from the point between B and C, the facile association of E, the general tendency to discuss several issues on different levels and to move from one to another without notice.

It may also strike the tutor that the general tone is unpretentious: there is very little reference to 'authorities' or to published work (contrast the probable content of an essay on the same subject). Whether this distresses him will depend on his preconceptions of what background knowledge his class 'should' have (though if they lack it, it is as well he should know this), and will depend also on the stage of the course reached. He may be pleased to note that where references to books are given they are relevant and well integrated into the discussion, and that there is a constant reference back to personal

* Detailed accounts of group meetings can be found in Thelen (1954), Woolf & Woolf (1957), Rogers (1951), Klein (1961), and Utterback (1953).

experiences (even occasionally overdone in anecdotes).*

There is a genuine attempt to deal with genuine problems, and at least two issues (factors associated with delinquency, and so-called moral deficiency) are discussed in some detail. One is left with the feeling, not that anything has been 'settled' (which one might have at the end of a lecture, and which is not particularly desirable), but that issues have been opened which some members may want to pursue. (Consider, for instance, the query of K and L, and the apparent readiness of B to read further).

Since a relatively large number of the group took an active part, it is reasonable to suppose that most of the discussion was at the level of the majority – not far above their heads, nor too remote to catch and hold attention – and that subsequently it will be remembered and linked with other work (remembered as meaningfully connected, not simply 'learned by heart'). Since the discussion is unpretentious, it is also unalarming, and since it goes along on several levels at once, it is open to each individual to identify himself with the level most suitable to him, without feeling superior or inferior or out of it altogether. (It is more difficult for a lecturer to appeal to several levels at once.) So the very diffuseness of the discussion is not wholly a disadvantage, or at least it can be turned to good account.

The tutor who has noticed the general level at which the group is functioning can then direct his attention to differences among individuals – the apparent superior ability of B, D, and G, for instance (is this confirmed on other occasions?) –'and can try to determine whether the less vocal ones are hampered by lack of information, inability to think clearly, few ideas, shyness, and so on. Contrast with this the lecturer who had nothing

---

* W. H. Whyte (1957, p. 49 ff.) makes some justifiable criticisms of the excessive glorification of 'consensus' and 'discussion'. He attacks the anti-intellectualism which advocates discussion methods merely as means for interaction, and which forgets that any course should be a discipline in its own right. I should make it clear that it is the genuineness and not the weaknesses of discussions that I am praising, and my position is not an anti-intellectualist one.

much to go on besides essays, which themselves gave a misleading picture, and the difference is clear.

Furthermore, as well as differences of ability, social and
attitudinal differences can be observed. There are, for example,
E's lack of confidence, G's popularity, and D's over-competitive-
ness. If the tutor is thinking of subdividing his group for particular purposes, G would seem to be a better choice as leader
than the diffident E or the unacceptable D – for though on
ability alone D might appear to have a strong claim, yet if his
effect is likely to be disruptive, it is better for the tutor to be
aware of this in advance and to think again.

I do not mean to suggest that the tutor jumps to conclusions
on the strength of this insufficient evidence, merely that he uses
it with the evidence from other occasions to construct a
developing picture of his group as people. Then, too, over a
period of time he can note if any changes are taking place – as,
for instance, a gradual building up of confidence in E, or an
increasing awareness on D's part that his manner puts people off
and a consequent readiness to try to tone it down. The example
hints at such changes, but obviously only a longer time can
show if in fact they are consistent trends.

It seems fair to conclude that methods which involve discussion have a great deal to commend them as an approach to
adult learning. They conform to the criteria suggested in the
previous chapter – How can we find the right level? How can we
provide situations that are meaningful to our students? How
can we ensure proper linkage between their present studies
and their past experience? How can we avoid unreal and passive
pseudo-learning?

I should next like to consider in some detail the part played
by the leader – how good intentions can be put into practice,
what his work involves, where things can begin to go wrong,
how discussions are prepared, guided, and consolidated, how
continuity is maintained, and so on.*

* See also *Discussion Method* (Bureau of Current Affairs, 1950).

Discussions do not just happen: they have to be worked for like anything else. It is a mistake to imagine that they make fewer demands on the tutor's knowledge of his subject, or that he can get by without preparation, or that the sum of several chaotic free-for-alls will miraculously form a coherent whole,* or that he can use them as his sole approach, to the exclusion of all lecturing and demonstrating. On the contrary, it is necessary to be clear at the beginning that the responsibility rests upon the tutor and that he abandons his lecture tram-lines at his peril, so he must be sure that whatever alternative he adopts will be profitable. The exploration of byways (see Leigh Hunt's essay 'The Graces and Anxieties of Pig-Driving') can be interesting and even instructive, but there must be some guarantee that the goal will be reached and that it is not (to continue the metaphor) the end of the Gadarene herd. It is the tutor's duty to know where he is going and to make sure that he gets there, otherwise he will merely have exchanged the tyranny of the syllabus for the tyranny of chaos. Incomprehensible incoherence is too heavy a price to pay even for the advantages mentioned, and it should be stressed that muddle and lack of continuity are the besetting sins of discussion situations. I have already criticized the acaedmic lecture with its proliferation of references, some valuable, some not, so that the students fail to see the wood for the trees; if the same confusion results from a series of discussions, nothing has been gained (except perhaps that the confusion in the students' minds is more obvious).

The tutor's preparation for discussions will differ in several respects from his procedure in preparing a set of lectures – but preparation there must be. He must know his subject, not merely in a straight line, so to speak, but backwards and sideways and round about. He is dealing not merely with a single strand, chosen and fully worked out in advance by himself, but with an interlocking whole in which the choices will be largely

* Compare Whyte's trenchant criticism of what he calls 'the intellectual hypocrisy of the leaderless group' (1957, p. 55).

Dis

made by others. It is therefore vital that he should be thoroughly familiar with his material and its interrelations, otherwise he will get lost himself, and then it will indeed be a case of the blind leading the blind. He needs not less knowledge of his subject, but more, since he has to see it in all its aspects and be able to orientate himself and his group from any angle. Suppose, for instance, a discussion reaches a point from which it may take

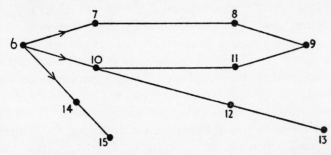

one of several paths. From 6 it may go via 7 and 8 or via 10 and 11. In either case 9 can be reached, and the choice may not matter very much. But at 10 there may be a further divergence, leading via 12 to 13, or the whole thing may go from 6 in quite a different direction to 14 and 15. Perhaps the tutor does not wish it to go to 15 and so takes avoiding action earlier – the point at issue here is that the tutor must know in advance what the likely lines of development are. Just as a chess player foresees the most probable combinations, so does the discussion leader: his preparation is general rather than specific, but in many ways it is more exacting than the preparation of a lecture. So many more things can go wrong, and it is not always possible to be forearmed.

After the preparation comes the actual discussion, and launching it can be quite a tricky business. Again, it is the tutor's responsibility to see that it gets off to a good start: once it has started, it gathers momentum, but the opening is usually chancy. I have found that it is generally best to begin myself with a short prepared statement, perhaps summarizing the point reached previously, perhaps mentioning alternative possibilities that are now ahead, perhaps choosing one topic and developing it until I am interrupted. Sometimes a member of the group starts straight away, for instance with a development of a point touched on at the last meeting, and in this case one has to think quickly whether it may lead on to a promising new line or is more likely to lead back to a repetition of previous topics: if the latter, the prepared statement will still be needed for a fresh start. There are times when the discussion fails to catch fire, and looking back afterwards one can see that the cause nearly always lies in an overhasty and inadequate introduction from the leader. It is not enough to announce a topic and leave it at that: some development, however brief, is required. Still less should the leader* start by saying, 'What are we going to talk about today?', for nothing gives a more haphazard impression of 'anything goes'. It is worth while devoting care and attention to the first five minutes, for the subsequent proceedings can be helped or jeopardized by the opening.

As the members take over, the leader can and should stay more in the background, and leave it to them as far as possible. His part, however, is still important, though it need not be obtrusive.

1. He can help to clarify statements where there is an element of doubt as to what is meant. Even if *he* thinks he knows what the speaker means, others may not, and perhaps are unwilling to admit this, so that he holds a watching brief on their behalf. Here his tone may be important, for to say 'Mr. X, do you mean this, or that, or the other?' in too magisterial a voice can be upsetting to X, and can convey unintentional overtones of impatience.

* The discussion leader need not always be the tutor. I have experimented with leaders from the group and have found that it worked well. On one occasion an unexpected visitor, a lecturer from another university, invited to take pot-luck at the discussion, thought the leader was a staff member. He was, in fact, one of the group. The size of the group at that discussion was between twenty and twenty-five.

2. The leader is responsible for seeing that the discussion does not wander *too* far from the point. He must have not only a sense of relevance, but also sufficient width of perception to tolerate something that, though not strictly relevant, is yet useful, and can be made relevant with a little broadening of the issue. It is wise to allow a little latitude, for often the byways are more interesting than the main road, yet to chase every red herring becomes frustrating to those who hope to 'get somewhere' at the end.

3. It is often wise to indicate explicitly the connections between points raised at different times, not only during one single discussion, but over a longer period, thus helping to give continuity: 'This agrees with what Miss M said', or 'That example could also be used in connection with what we were discussing a fortnight ago', or 'If we follow that up, it may suggest a different conclusion from the one we reached before', or 'How far does that fit in with Mrs. N's standpoint?', or 'Those of you who come from country districts may be able to give us some first-hand examples here.'

4. Some of the sentences above refer not only to the past but also to the future, suggesting what *may* be done now or later. That is, the leader is not merely linking, he is also guiding and steering. Further examples of this can be found at the beginning of the chapter: the tutor intervenes to underline D's suggestion, so that it will not go for nothing, but he goes further than D has actually gone. This could nevertheless be considered as an interpretation of D's meaning, and D accepts it as such. However, his second intervention goes further than free interpretation and says, in effect, 'Don't let us deal with technical offences'. No doubt he is wise in that, because he hopes to keep the discussion in profitable channels, but it is a definite piece of steering, as is his later attempt to rescue J. How far a leader should go in encouraging or discouraging certain issues is a debatable point and will vary with the situation; but probably most people would agree

that the two extremes of *laissez faire* and over-direction are both to be avoided. On some occasions he may need to say quite firmly, 'We're not going into that!' – but this is a dangerous habit. Here again his tone will count as much as his actual words, and, as I hoped to show by the exclamation mark, it need not be dogmatic even if his words are.

5. The question of disagreement is one that must be dealt with separately. It is a poor discussion where there are no differences of opinion, and one suspects that there is a lack of frankness and that the apparent unity is only a façade. There is usually something to be said on several sides of any important matter, and it is most desirable that they should all be stated. Indeed, it is one particular advantage of the discussion method over a lecture that it avoids the smoothing and over-simplification which may result when one individual deals with a controversial topic. Even if he attempts to show more than one side, he may end up with a list of advantages and disadvantages, but all, so to speak, along one dimension. By contrast, the results of a discussion cannot easily be so reduced: they tend to spatter out into several dimensions. This gives a stereoscopic effect of depth and is valuable in counteracting the superficial notion that there are pat 'answers' to all 'problems', and that these have only to be found and then learned by heart. It is an important discovery when a student realizes that his pet solution is not the only one, that the factors to be considered are complex and may be incommensurable.*

However, the appearance of widely different and possibly irreconcilable points of view puts a strain on tolerance and charity, and can lead to dissensions within the group, especially if some of the members are rather immature and inclined to take things personally. As Knowlson (1951, p. 9)

* Hippasos of Metapontion was drowned for divulging the incommensurability of the side of a square with its diagonal – which cut at the whole basis of the Orphic system of philosophy.

wisely said, 'Adults must learn to distinguish between people and ideas, and to challenge ideas without threatening people', and it is a useful function of a discussion to provide training in tolerance of unacceptable ideas.* Here the leader has to try to set the tone, and to see to it that disputes do not become acrimonious and personal. Usually prevention is better than cure, and, by building up an easy-going atmosphere in which it is taken as a matter of course that not everyone will think alike, the tutor can hope to avoid serious dissensions. 'There seem to be several points of view here', said in a matter-of-fact tone and as if it is a perfectly acceptable and unsurprising situation, is probably better than an attempt to overcome the differences. The latter, when it does not succeed, suggests that there is something disgraceful in disagreement: it is the emotional overtone which is damaging. Of course it is reasonable to seek common ground wherever possible but, if it cannot be found, that is that, and the less fuss the better. On the rare occasions when personal attacks do occur, it is often wise to turn a blind eye and allow the incidents to subside of their own accord, but this must depend on the judgement of the tutor. There has been only a single occasion when I felt that intervention from me was called for, though in fact I did not intervene. Y and Z had bickered at each other for weeks and finally Y overstepped all bounds with a sudden unprovoked attack on Z: I was too surprised to act at the time, but determined not to let anything further pass. From that day forward there were no more attacks, but how or why I cannot explain. Possibly the problem had worked itself out, or possibly the rest of the very united group had stepped in.

6. I have suggested that differing or alternative explanations can have the effect of enriching the students' understanding. The complexity of pattern does, however, mean that the

* Compare Voltaire's famous defence of free speech, even in a cause which he disliked.

leader must be alert all the time to the ramifications and interrelations of the various contributions, otherwise he and his group will get lost. To refer back to the diagram on p. 57, 6 could lead to 7, 8, 9, or to 10, 11, 9, or to 10, 12, 13, or to 14, 15. Let us supppose that it has in fact gone along 7, 8, 9. At this point, 0 comes in with 12. Evidently he (and possibly some others) has been thinking along the lines 6, 10, 12, while the discussion has ranged along 7, 8, and 9. If the leader does nothing, 0's contribution may simply pass unnoticed and the discussion will continue on its previous lines, or it may start a new line, leaving the old one to wither and die. (As an example of this, see E's intervention in the discussion at the beginning of the chapter.) If, however, the leader feels that one line is likely to be much more profitable than the other, he will probably reinforce that line; or, better, he will not treat them as disjunctives but will try to show the relationship between them. For instance, he may make explicit the connection with the starting-point 6, via 10, and then encourage a transition from 10 to 11, and so a return to 9. In this way, 0's contribution has been woven into the general fabric, and both routes to 9 (via 7 and 8, and via 10 and 11) have been used. Thus, both those who associated along the original line 7, 8, 9, and those whose associations were like 0's, have been satisfied; and each group's line has been explained to the other. Alternatively, the leader may feel that 9 has been sufficiently dealt with and that 12 can be a useful growing-point leading on to 13 and beyond, and so while he stresses its relevance to the previous issue he may be very glad to encourage the new topic. The leader, then, orientates the discussion and provides guideposts so that the members understand the connections between the various points. Remembering that a discussion of necessity has a complex structure, he seeks to interpret that structure wherever there is likely to be difficulty or misunderstanding.

It is worth while making a comparison here with the structure of a set lecture, which has a single line of thought selected for it by the lecturer. This may not, however, be the natural line of thought of several of the listeners, and their associations are constantly going off the trail and having to be brought back. Since the lecturer does not know what o and his like are thinking, he cannot help, and so unless o can integrate his sidelines himself, they remain unintegrated. Not only is a source of richness lost, but also o may be confused as to how things fit in and the lecturer is unaware of this confusion. A discussion *seems* more confused, because the difficulties are brought to the surface; the lecturer sails placidly along on the smooth current of his own thought, but all his hearers' difficulties lie below.

7. It is worth remembering that silence can be valuable. A member may not be taking part in the discussion and yet may be following it intently and doing a lot of thinking of his own. It is the quality, and not the amount, of the contribution that counts. Naturally the leader will wish to have as many of the group as possible joining in, but that will not be his sole, nor his chief, criterion of the success of a discussion. There is no value in people talking just for the sake of talking. As the leader gets to know his group better, he will have an idea of the reasons why some are hesitant to join in, and will use his judgement as to when it is or is not wise to encourage their participation. Certainly an issue should never be made of it, but with good sense and tact, and an easy atmosphere in the discussion, sooner or later most members will find that they have a contribution to make, and will gain confidence thereby.

Sometimes the whole group falls silent and an inexperienced leader may find this worrying. Before he rushes into the gap, however, he is wise to stop and ask himself what is causing the silence. Is it one of emptiness, where the members are as embarrassed as he is himself and do not know

63

how to act? Or is it that they are busy thinking? – it would be a pity to interrupt in that case, for valuable contributions frequently follow such a silence. Or it may be that the matter under discussion has reached its natural ending and the members are, so to speak, rounding it off in their minds before turning to a new subject. Prolonged silence, of course, is embarrassing: but I think most tutors err in the under-use rather than the over-use of silence.

8. As time passes and the group settles down, many of the functions of the leader will gradually be taken over by the members. For instance, they will themselves develop a sense of relevance and will call to order those who wander too far from the point; at the same time, with widening tolerance of differing views, they may be more ready to consider minority opinions. As they get to know each other better, they will encourage the diffident, temper the wind to the shorn lamb, and tone down the over-ebullient. Again, as they see more clearly the general pattern, so it will be easier for them to relate new work to what has gone before and to provide their own signposts. As one student put it: 'When I get a bright idea, instead of rushing out with it, I have to stop and think how far it will fit in with what other people are saying and how best I can put it into words so that I will not waste their time and yet so that it will be clear and not cause misunderstandings. I find it a terrific discipline for myself.' Another said briefly: 'I ask myself (a) is it accurate? (b) is it important? (c) is it relevant?' When this happens, the tutor can feel that the discussions have provided practical training in clear thinking, have encouraged tolerance and sensitivity to the needs of others, and in these respects have been genuinely educative.

Next, we have to consider how discussions can be used to the best advantage, followed up, and consolidated. In the example at the beginning of the chapter the students went out arguing, and probably they were interested and stimulated – but probably, too, their notebooks were almost empty. It is difficult to take notes and at the same time join actively in a discussion, and though note-taking in many classes is overdone (witness a large number of current jokes), on the other hand there must be some permanent record of the work done. Adults like to feel that they have got something out of the time, and though six pages of notes after a lecture may be a barren triumph if there is little understanding of their meaning, yet to have none at all is rather discouraging. Memory fades, and an hour which seemed stimulating at the time soon appears empty in retrospect if the notebook is also empty.

The issue must be faced honestly by tutors and some compromise reached: for instance, some groups like to have a summing up in the last five minutes of the meeting (either by the tutor or by one of their number), and during that time pens are furiously busy. Others like to appoint a reporter at the beginning of the hour, who takes down what is said, arranges it at his leisure to bring out the salient points (often very difficult, considering the complex structure of most discussions), and makes a report available to the group in time for it to be studied before the next meeting, particularly if the topics follow in sequence. Alternatively, each member may write up his own recollections as soon as possible after the discussion hour. Each method has its own advantages and drawbacks. The summary has the advantage of immediacy, but it is often difficult for one person to do justice to all that has been said without time for reflection. The reporter has time for reflection and he has full notes at his disposal, but obviously a good deal depends on his competence since everyone's eggs are put into his basket. Perhaps he is the sort of person who would not want to enter into a discussion, and as reporter his gifts are utilized for the benefit of the group, so that he can feel he is doing his bit. Both these methods have in common that one single pattern is presented to the group. I tend to prefer the diversity of the

65

third method, where each member makes his own summary and takes from the discussion what has interested *him*, but this procedure may be too difficult for some. If it is used, the tutor should explicitly draw the attention of the group to the need for a permanent record, not leaving it to chance whether or not they make up their notes, and he should be ready to help where it is required. A wise course is to employ more than one method according to the occasion.

The tutor himself must scrutinize carefully what has and what has not been covered in the discussion, particularly since it will not have followed as straightforward a pattern as a lecture would have done. Several bites may have been taken at several cherries. Some topics may have been considered more deeply than another which was just touched upon, and which will therefore need further consideration later. (Should the tutor deal with this in a brief set talk, or leave the subject to come up again in discussion from another angle so that it can be seen in the round, or actively steer a later discussion to make sure that it *is* raised again?) In effect, he is widening his time-scale, ensuring that, say, six topics will be covered satisfactorily in six weeks, but not at an even rate of one per week. Obviously this makes it harder for the tutor to keep track of the proceedings, and so it is more than ever necessary that he should know what he is doing. Because this way of working appears less methodical, he himself must be more so. For instance, suppose three hours are available for the consideration of delinquency, and one of these has been used in the discussion cited, the remaining time can be spent in further discussions (in which case the tutor must see that aspects other than those already raised are adequately dealt with) or in straight lecturing (if he thinks that factual information is now the prime need of the group). Thus his planning is a continuing process, modified to meet the demands of the changing scene, and mindful of the need for consolidation.

Consolidation can be sought in many ways. A discussion can

be followed up by one or more straight lectures; or by the collection of information gained through interviews, practical work, or visits; or by reading. The aim is that the student should see meaning and purpose in all that he does, and that he should clearly understand its relevance for him. A discussion that was not very satisfactory in the tutor's opinion may still be a better starting-point to further endeavour, if the student liked and understood it, than a more competent and scholarly lecture whose value was not clear to the student. Whatever its limitations, the discussion has got home to him, has caught him where he is, and so he is prepared to move on from that point. Let us suppose that he requires factual confirmation or disproof of rather wide generalizations made in the discussion. Some of these facts he can get at first-hand, from his own visits and observations, but others require more prolonged searching. He may try to consult other people, perhaps by interview at the Citizens' Advice Bureau, or by enquiry at the Town Hall, or by asking his colleagues at work. The facts he wants may be written down in the Borough Handbook, or in the Medical Officer's Report, or in textbooks. He can now see the need for reading; it is not simply an external requirement which he will do if he has to, without fully realizing in what ways it is going to help him.

It is, in fact, much easier to get adults to consolidate their studies in orthodox ways (by the use of the library and so on) than might at first appear. The precondition of success is that the basis *from which they start* shall be solidly grounded and comprehensible to them. If we provide plenty of hooks by which their work can be linked firmly to their past experience and present needs, the problem of consolidating is well on the way to solution. I have already quoted Peers as saying that discussion of 'problems' is useless without informed knowledge; although this is true,* the answer is certainly not to pump in

* I would not for a moment wish to suggest that discussion alone is the be-all and end-all.

academic knowledge *ad nauseam*. As long as the 'knowledge' is seen as remote, it will remain inert; the better way is to start at the other end, from the avowed interests and concerns of the students. To build slowly and firmly, on a sound foundation of comprehension, is in the long run the wisest policy. The 'facts' can come later – and they will come, too, for, *given a valid motive for learning*, adult students are immensely hard workers and very ready to fill in gaps in their information. 'The letter killeth, but the spirit giveth life.' The spirit that we want to foster is one of interest and understanding. If each, at his own level, knows what he is doing, there is a good chance that he will go forward from that, consolidating as he goes. 'To cover the syllabus' is not a valid motive for learning, but when they have a sound motive adults will cover the syllabus all the same and with much more depth of understanding.

In the final section of this chapter, I should like to consider briefly numbers, pace, and varying capabilities.

It is often stated that discussion groups of eight to fifteen people are the most satisfactory from the point of view of size; however, many adult classes exceed these numbers. The tutor has then to choose whether he will attempt to run discussions with his larger group in spite of the difficulties, or forgo their advantages (assuming that he cannot divide his class). I have experimented with discussion groups of up to thirty people and have no hesitation in saying that they *can* be worked. A teaching lecture can well replace a set lecture at this size, and may be a desirable first step; after that, it is possible to try occasional discussions with an ordinary-sized lecture class and see how things go, gradually increasing their frequency if they are successful. Obviously there will be less opportunity for individual contributions, a more unwieldy structure, and a greater chance of the discussion getting out of hand, than in a more orthodox-sized group; but at least individual opportunities will be greater than in a set lecture. At the same time, the larger group makes demands on the leader's skill and raises problems related to the differing capabilities – and I use this word to include personal qualities as well as ability – of the members.

The pace of a discussion is in one sense slower than that of a teaching lecture, and the latter is slower than a set lecture. It might appear that the abler members would become bored when less ground has been covered in the time, but it is not as simple as that, for more than one dimension is involved; as well as the overall pace of material, there is the speed with which contributions succeed each other to be considered. The latter may be quite rapid, and rather confusing when a number of slightly different aspects of a subject are raised in succession. From that point of view, it is often the quicker, livelier, more extraverted members who are most stimulated by discussion, while others find it unsatisfactory and muddling. An able person who is not irritated (some are) by the diffuseness of a discussion may gain considerably from its variety and the rapid succession of points of view. A slower person also may be irritated by the diffuseness, though for a different reason, because he fears he may not be able to sort it out; this is a risk, but my impression is that the slower members stand to profit on the whole by the freedom to ask when they do not understand and by having their work brought home to them thoroughly. As I write, I have before me a number of statements from old students which make these points, and there is no straightforward relationship between ability as such and satisfaction or dissatisfaction with discussion as a means of learning. I would say that the great advantage of discussion is that *all* can take from it and contribute to it at their own level, and the differences between individuals (both temperamental and intellectual) are more fully allowed for than in a lecture situation. It is a more exciting situation for the tutor who is interested in people, but it is also, because of its very complexity, more chancy. 'Some of the most stimulating discussions arose quite accidentally and without preparation, say, at morning breaks and lunch-times, whereas some of the least successful and most artificial appeared to be those where we were previously informed that such and such a topic would be discussed at a certain date' (F.S.).

There are more things to go wrong in a discussion, and one can never be sure, as one can with a well-prepared lecture, of a smooth passage. Vigilance, tact, care, and forethought on the part of the tutor can decrease the chances of confusion, and small points, such as seating arrangements so that everybody can see everybody else, can help, but the risk remains. If the tutor and his class feel that the game is worth the candle, then they will be ready to take what is, in essence, a calculated risk.

I shall end by quoting at length from two of the statements mentioned above, each of which gives a balanced summary from the members' point of view, thus pulling together the argument of this and the preceding chapter.

A. 'Having been enthusiastic all the year about discussions, I have previously thought little about lectures to the group, taking this method for granted. In my case I think *enjoyment* was equal. Some *feel* they learn more from one, some from the other, and a mixture seems a good thing.

'Lectures can build up one attitude in the group, who can pour out of the room saying *"wasn't* that exciting!", "interesting", "I was fascinated!" There is a tendency during coffee to savour the outstanding picture or points, and unless it has been deliberately provocative it is often some time before questions arise or thoughts travel outwards from it. The group can be receptive like a child hearing a story and does not want – at first – to move away from or break down what it has enjoyed.

'The members of the group either listen to and soak up what is said and the attitudes or feelings towards it, letting their minds wander down channels suggested by the lecture (and back to it!) and go off with a colourful picture but misty details; or they aim at getting down the facts, writing full notes – every point they feel must be learned and remembered. The first tend to note salient points or odd phrases that will recall certain trends of thought – they often find that they have "never thought of that before" or that things "fall into place" because of the way they have been presented, and it is not necessary to write detailed notes of these things; they have been made aware of something that they really knew and that leads so obviously and logically from something previously known that it will in future be remembered or at least easily recalled by similar trains of thought without deliberate making and learning of notes.

'I find that my notes taken in lectures contain many words and phrases that are not my own. These might increase vocabulary or, if they were deliberately "learned", lead to use of jargon.

'During a lecture to a small group, politeness forbids asking one's neighbour to explain, e.g. a simple term used by the lecturer and not known to the student – the next few minutes can be most confusing! A beginner among the experienced may refrain from asking during question-time since others will not be interested and, again, such questions may seem impolite–but it is often surprising how many experienced people will gladly listen to question and answer at coffee-time.

'Discussions allow question and answer between neighbours and less is lost through lack of understanding.

'Some say they find the exchange of many ideas bewildering; others enjoy listening to the discussion and find it gives a wide and vivid picture, though they say they think too slowly to put their comments into words. They can appreciate different viewpoints, though.

'On the whole, all students, and particularly those who are "beginners" as students and have come to "be taught", learn from a good straight lecture and enjoy it. Those with more experience or who want to fill in gaps, etc., and enjoy discussions, get more from discussions than the beginners – but one of the advantages to the talkative type is the exercise of trying to think quickly and clearly and put in a useful query

71

Educating Older People

or remark at the right time, making it striking and clear and *short*' (F.S.).

B. '1. Lectures are useful for some things – putting across facts. Less chance of waste of time with lectures, at least on the surface – who knows what goes on underneath? Lectures can be inspirational, too. I never felt that listening to a good lecture was other than active learning. Often more satisfying than discussion and often more actively involving. Lectures which incorporate some discussion are useful for maintaining contact – such lectures broke off naturally into discussion quite frequently. In one sense I would say that they were discussions where we did a lot of listening. There were times when it was obvious that it would break contact and destroy the continuity of what was coming across if we interrupted, but I think most of the time we felt perfectly at ease to ask a question or to put a different viewpoint in the middle of it all. I would still call them lectures primarily, though. On the whole, I think I learn most from that kind of thing; the stimulus is greater than in discussion, general discussion that is. It occurs to me now that not only would you accept questions and other points of view in the middle of lectures but would take time to follow them out and in doing so change the course of the lecture. The lecture might then become "discursive" in nature but I would say still essentially unchanged in character. What gives it the character of a lecture? It seems to me that the essence of the lecture is that you have a situation where one person brings very much more than the others to the consideration of some thing, idea, problem, and has also prepared, so to speak, a brief. Discussion, on equal terms, would be a waste of time and in fact could not occur. Whether or not the lecturer permits, encourages, provokes discussion then becomes purely a matter of tactics – how best to get it over? I don't think the argument has become circular because I've asked that question. That kind of discussion would, to me, be part of the lecture. Conditions for it to occur successfully: a small class, some

72

relationship already established, a lecturer with good command of the subject and well able to control the situation. Much better than pure lecture – I would say for everything.*

'2. Discussions are useful for finding out attitudes and showing to all the realities of differing viewpoints. (How can he believe that? But there he does.) What do I mean here by discussions? I mean consideration of some thing, etc., by a group on equal terms as far as opportunity to speak and status are concerned.

'[Discussion is] necessary when considering situations new to everybody – unless in a strictly authoritarian setting. [It is also] necessary when putting over important things that have no demonstrable proof . . . gives people the chance to make up their own minds. Avoids reaction. But true discussion demands openmindedness all round, i.e. we must all be prepared to learn from discussion.

'[It is] desirable, therefore, only to use discussion when a large majority have something to contribute and when the matter is debatable. As an extreme example, it would be a waste of time for facts to be treated by discussion. You taught us those: we could question and receive an answer and re-question, but that did not make it discussion. Now for another example, this time the very opposite of an extreme one, where it may have looked very much like a discussion but was in fact essentially a lecture. You summed up the discussion and I've got it down as quite sharp conclusions. Looking at the conclusions now they're part of my outlook. But they weren't then, neither did I have the experience or ability to assess them. It wasn't discussion that made them right for me, though they seemed reasonable enough, but your saying so. But it helped that they had been talked about and agreed by others. I feel sure that if the "discussion" had resulted in other conclusions you wouldn't have endorsed them. In the sense that you guided the talking, got out what I think you wanted, stopped it at a convenient point,

* This is what I previously called a 'teaching lecture' (p. 41).

and then gave it back to us, I'd say that there was a lecture and not a discussion.

'An example of a discussion: you asked how people think, how they arrive at conclusions, solve problems, etc. We all had different ideas here – logical steps, flashes of insight, intuition, etc. – and you listened to it all, giving equal value to all suggestions. Here I think we all learned. You didn't sum up; we'd talked around it and that was that.

'3. As I've been writing, the thought has been forming that perhaps as adults we continue to learn in much the same ways as children, and that division of our further education into lectures and discussion doesn't really happen. We learn through contact with a teacher and by cooperating in the work planned for us, sometimes listening, sometimes talking, sometimes performing. How much we learn will depend on how much the teacher has to give, on the reality of the contact and communication, and on how much we are prepared to and can accept. Satisfaction of basic needs will have an influence on the last two factors. I never felt that anything was cut and dried on the course. We didn't learn solely through lectures or discussion, or best by one or the other but by a whole process comprised of many things. Teaching?' (F.S.).

Chapter Five

SUPERVISION OF PRACTICAL WORK

MANY COURSES for adults, particularly those with a vocational relevance, contain an element of practical work: thus a course for teachers may involve work in school, health visitors are required to take classes in parent-craft, social workers of various kinds undertake visiting or interviewing, and so on. This practical work is extremely valuable in counteracting any tendency to theoretical learning alone, and at the same time the theoretical studies give, or should give, point and meaning to experiences which the student may have had before without precisely realizing their significance (for instance, insights gained from lectures and discussions can help a teacher in dealing with difficulties of learning or of behaviour that formerly he avoided). In some cases the work itself is new – for example, an initial training course in teaching undertaken by an older person; in other cases the student is already qualified or experienced, and is specializing now in a particular branch – for example, a trained social worker who wishes to become a psychiatric social worker. The first is likely to be more obviously unsure of what he is doing, and there may be difficulties if the contrast with his adult state and general competence and maturity is not recognized by those in authority; the second knows the ropes, at least generally, and any difficulties that arise are likely to be more subtle. In either case, the supervision of the work of one adult by another raises issues which are

75

different from those when the trainee is a young person, and this is quite apart from any *technical* difficulties concerning the actual competence of the student.

It is surprising that so little should have been written about supervision: for myself, I have found most help in *Social Service and Mental Health* by Ashdown and Brown (1953) – which goes to reinforce my point that different disciplines can learn much from each other and that comparable problems exist in several professions. In what follows, though I shall write mainly with experienced teachers in view, yet I believe there is much that has relevance in other situations.

If practical work is to be done, it is desirable that it should also be supervised, if possible. Perhaps the word 'supervision' may sound unacceptable; but the reality behind the word need not be. If it is thought of positively and constructively, it becomes an opportunity for two people to get together and talk shop. Assuming that both are interested in the technical problems of their profession, they will find, in the supervision of practical work, a common meeting ground in what has happened on a particular occasion, and concrete examples by which they can test what has previously been discussed in the lecture room.

To give a personal example, I find that the real teaching of a series on 'remedial reading' is never done in the lectures but in individual tutorials, taking the work which the student has done with actual children as examples. If I had not seen these children being taught, this would not be possible. It may be that the tasks set for a child were too easy or too hard, or not really interesting for the particular child;* or perhaps work with one child went swimmingly and with another failed, although in both cases it had been imaginatively and carefully planned; or perhaps a suggestion had been taken over from a previous discussion but an essential element had been missed, and so on.

---

* The essence of remedial teaching is that the work set should be tailor-made to fit each individual.

Without seeing what happened one can only speculate why things went right or wrong, and although a supervisor's visits can be only occasional, it would be a pity if one never saw what happened. By going to look, one can see the level on which a student is actually functioning, and one must know this level in order to be able to help him. There is a tremendous range among our adult students, and it is not possible to make an accurate estimation of the operational level from seeing a student in college, even in relatively free situations such as discussions. One always gets shocks! Here is one man, for instance, whose work in all respects is excellent; another has equally attractive apparatus, but not much contact with the children. If they both brought their materials and records to a seminar, they would appear equally good, and the limitations of the second would not be realized and therefore would not be dealt with. A third may start off at a much lower level, but over a period of time make considerable advance; and a fourth and fifth may be very much better or worse in a teaching situation than would have been anticipated from their reactions outside.

The visit, then, can be useful both to student and to tutor. The student who has been working with John and Mary and Richard would rather discuss *them* than listen exclusively to generalized statements, of which a lecture necessarily consists (or, if it gives examples, they may not be applicable to John). If I had not seen John and Mary, I would hesitate to commit myself ('it might be this, or that, or the other'), and such tentative comment, though it is all that I can in honesty offer, is of limited help. To say, 'If you point out those children that you are particularly concerned about, I'll have a good look at them when I come', is at least to offer the possibilities of consultation, and two heads are better than one. The student may be glad to know that he is not the only person who thinks Richard a very difficult little boy, and that I agree that in admittedly imperfect circumstances the best possible is being done. He may feel disappointed that I could not produce a startlingly effective solution, but on reflection it may seem to him that perhaps he is not doing so badly after all, and that perhaps some problems have not got solutions, or at least not easily discoverable ones – both of which reflections may be quite salutary.

From my side, it is helpful to me to know the situation with which the student is actually confronted and to try to assess the elements of strength or weakness that are displayed. For instance, is the work suitable, well-graded, attractive? Does Mr. Smith seem at ease with children of this age? Is he better with boys than with girls? Is he rather pedestrian or does he show imagination? Is he technically competent? Granted that Richard is very difficult, is Mr. Smith over-anxious about him? Does he tend to drive for results? What is his reaction to nervous, aggressive, or slow children? These are but some of the many questions that occur, and from them a picture of the situation may be built up. It is not by any means an accurate picture, being based on a sample only, a particular day; but such as it is, it is probably much better than one that could be obtained by indirect means only, by reports, records, and apparatus.

Reports from a third person have the disadvantage that one cannot always tell what his presuppositions and standards are, and that he may be unwilling, especially if the report is a written one, to commit himself to any unfavourable comment. Furthermore, it is difficult to collate a number of such reports, and so different individuals may be judged in fact on different qualities and at varying standards.

Records of the students themselves are useful, but are not entirely reliable as a guide to performance:

1. Those who are not very good at expressing themselves on paper are penalized.
2. Full and detailed records show the depth of the student's understanding; but scrappy ones can have opposite interpre-

tations – a really skilful teacher may have less need to put down details of preparation than one who is learning on the job, or records may be scrappy because the teacher has limited understanding of what is required.

3. It is easier for records to give an accurate picture of the work projected or covered than of the contact between teacher and children, yet the latter is vital in a remedial teaching situation.

4. In rare cases records may be unintentionally misleading – a neurotic teacher projected some of his own characteristics on to the children, and his records bore little relation to the children when one actually met them, but from reading alone one would have thought the records remarkably perceptive and cohesive.

5. On one occasion only I have known records to be 'cooked'.

Materials and apparatus show the technical skill of the teacher and his grasp of teaching steps, but it is the *use* made of the apparatus that counts, not the apparatus itself, however excellent.

The nature of this example from a teaching situation may make it a particularly favourable one, but much the same advantages may follow from the discussion of practical work entailed by supervision in other situations. The crux of the matter seems to me to turn on what the supervision is intended to do: is it thought of as derogatory to adult dignity, a mere looking for faults; or is it thought of positively as an opportunity for consultation, advice, and help? Two comments follow at this point: though they may appear in some ways contradictory I think that both are applicable, and they complicate the issue which I have rather over-simplified so far.

First, it is possible for a student to realize that supervision is an 'opportunity for help',* to welcome and invite it con-

* In what follows I am assuming that this is in fact the case, and except for one example I shall say nothing about the merely carping supervisor, though I admit that he can exist.

sciously, and at the same time to be dubious of it or hostile to it subconsciously. It is too simple to say that all one has to do as a supervisor is honestly to offer help, for all difficulties to be removed: it must be recognized that adults have attitudes which are often firmly set, and that previous experience may have conditioned them to be suspicious of anything that appears like authority. Even when the supervisor does not adopt an overtly critical air, the fact that he can say 'this is good' may be nearly as difficult for some people to stomach as if he had said 'this is bad'; in either case, a judging situation is involved, and 'who is he to judge me?' may be the unspoken and possibly unconscious reaction. (A very fair comment, we should do well to remind ourselves: who *are* we to judge another?) Where the student is a beginner, the fact that he is adult may make him resentful of correction, because it is a threat to his adult status. Where the student is considerably experienced in the field of his study, the position is still more ticklish, particularly if he is taking a vocational course which may affect his livelihood; he has already a good deal of self-esteem invested in his status as a teacher or social worker, and anything that appears to cut at that esteem (as even favourable comment can do) can be a considerable threat to security.

The second comment is this: on the whole, one meets more difficulty from students who wish for *more* direction than they are given, than from those who resent advice. How far this is an artifact, the result of one's own attitude, it is difficult to say, but certainly life is not all honey for the non-directive tutor. 'He's a beast! He won't help me', flared one adult after visiting her tutor. 'Yes, he was quite nice when he gave my work back and said it was good, but when I asked him what I should do next he wouldn't tell me but said I should decide for myself.' The cross-currents in this case require a bit of straightening out. There may be some resentment at the inferior position involved in being told that her work is good. Against this, there is a considerable desire for a *more* dependent position than the tutor is prepared to allow. It is a chastening thought to the conscientiously non-directive tutor that he may be creating more insecurity by demanding an independence of judgement for which this student is apparently not ready. Or is it simply that she has formed such a strong stereotype as to how persons in authority 'should' behave* that she clamours for it – but would not particularly relish it if she got it. Here the absence of direction is equated with lack of interest: it is seen as a withholding of something that the tutor *could* give.

It might be expected that the first reaction would be commoner among aggressive, the second among over-compliant, personalities. But there is a further complication, that both together may operate in the same person and produce an uneasy swinging from one extreme to another. Such a student will positively *demand*, in aggressive tones, that he be told exactly what to do; and yet one can surmise only too readily, from the aggression boiling up just below the surface, what the result would be if his request were complied with. I should make it clear that I am not including here the relatively simple situation where the unsureness is a direct and very natural result of not knowing what to do: some straightforward help is the obvious reply to that situation. I am considering the student whose ability and knowledge are amply sufficient, but although he *could* find his own solution, he does not *feel* that he could, that is, his anxiety and insecurity get in the way of using his considerable abilities. Direct advice in this case only feeds the resentment (it appears like patronage) and at the same time increases the insecurity (that it should be thought to be necessary); in the last resort, only the experience of finding his own solution, and the confidence that comes from the realization that he *can* do so, are likely to help such a student. But the last resort is not the present situation, and the immediate expedient presents the tutor with an awkward choice of evils.†

* She was a member of a strongly authoritarian sect.
† For a full working out of this kind of situation, see the example of Mrs. Severn in Chapters 8 and 9 of this book.

To turn now to the supervisor, the picture is complicated from his side too. An honest desire to do the best he can for his students may be the beginning of his armour, but it is by no means the end, and he, too, just as the students, may have attitudes and needs that exert their effect on his dealings with them, not necessarily in ways that he would consciously wish. Since he is working with people, his own personality becomes an important factor in the total situation, whether or not he recognizes this fact. If he does not recognize it, he will get along happily with some and antagonize others; but the 'disciplined use of his own personality'* can considerably increase his effectiveness. In all work with people, it is never sufficient to be an expert in whatever-it-may-be: what you are is at least as important as what you know. It is possible to be a competent mathematician and be blundering and bossy in one's dealings with others, or a scientist and have little idea of how to get through to others; as supervisors, such people would fail in effectiveness, however knowledgeable they might be in their own subjects. A certain humility of approach is essential, and the cocksure person who *knows* he is right, even if he is right, will not get very far. This suggests, then, that supervision calls for qualities of personal skill which are akin to those of the almoner, the probation officer, the welfare worker; that, in fact, much can be learned from the approach of the skilled social worker. Ashdown and Brown (1953)† try to pin down the qualities of personality that are advantageous to a worker and those that can hamper him in his dealings with others; their interesting discussion is most suggestive in a wider context than that which they are considering, the selection of the professional social worker.

In later chapters it will be necessary to inquire more deeply into this matter of 'skill with people', but for our present purposes it is sufficient simply to note that supervision can fruitfully

* Ashdown & Brown (1953, p. 149).
† See Chapter 4.

be regarded as a special example of social work visiting, that similarly requires tact, forbearance, and tolerance.

In calling attention to things which may go wrong and in stressing that good intentions alone are not enough, it is necessary to avoid giving an extreme picture of so many difficulties and drawbacks that the tutor is afraid to move. I hope I have not done this: it would be a pity to suggest that ordinary good human relations are so difficult to establish and maintain. There is a sort of 'beginner's luck' by which an unreflective but naturally pleasant and friendly supervisor can get by for some time, and the fact that he does not see the possibilities of tension and friction can help more than if he saw them and was scared of them! Later, let us hope, his luck will be replaced by skill, for without the latter it cannot last. But skill of what sort? What does the supervisor do? Let us try to break down the general statement of his function 'to help the student' into its component parts, proceeding from the straightforward to the more complicated.

First, the provision of direct suggestion and advice. This is the most obvious function, and I shall say nothing about it: it is to be assumed that the supervisor is competent and that his advice is sensible and sound. Direct advice, however, can have an unfortunate side-effect if it cuts at the security of the student, on the lines discussed earlier.

Second, discussion as between professional equals. The attempt here is to play down the authority angle which, as we saw, can create difficulties, and to substitute instead a straightforward consultation such as the student might have with one of his colleagues. It is admitted that students learn a lot from one another, partly, perhaps, because the barriers are down and there is none of the prickliness that can appear in the face of authority; if only this relaxed attitude can be reproduced with the supervisor, it is argued, it will be easier for the student to learn. There is a great deal in this, but of course it depends on the 'if only', and the condition may be unrealizable – at least it is a worthwhile aim. Such an approach has the big advantage that it implies the competence of the student, and so it is particularly suitable in the case of older and experienced persons. The supervisor limits himself to considering with the student the pros and cons of each possible line of action, leaving the decision to the student. He is likely to have, so to speak, a map of the territory, and his expertise consists not in saying 'go this way' but in displaying it as a whole and its related parts. This method may sound tentative, and it can seem so to students who would prefer a cut-and-dried objective, but in appropriate cases it can work well.

In this context, 'appropriate cases' are selected on grounds of temperament as well as of ability. For instance, a determined and independent adult may prefer to work out his own solution in a field which is new to him, even though from his previous lack of experience he might seem a suitable candidate for direct advice. As a general rule, no doubt, those who are more experienced can carry greater responsibility for decision than those who are undertaking a new venture, but it is by no means universal. The mere likelihood of floundering and failing is not in itself a reason for intervention* from the supervisor, providing the failure is not going to be too discouraging, for often one learns most from taking one's own line and failing in it, continuing, and perhaps finally succeeding. A man who had a large number of bright ideas, but who was rather inclined to woolliness and vagueness of detail, came with a grandiose scheme to his tutor. The various possibilities (the 'map of the territory') were discussed with him and the likelihood of confusion mentioned, but no attempt was made to dissuade him – it was his responsibility. A week later he came in and said cheerfully and ruefully (if this is not a contradiction) 'I'm up a gum tree'. The following week it was 'I've climbed further up my gum tree'. But it was *his* gum tree and he was willing to accept it, and it was not damaging to him to admit that his

* After all, we all once learned to walk.

ideas had not succeeded; rather, the experience had been useful to him and he would use it profitably in the future.* The stage of floundering and uncertainty, as Ashdown and Brown point out,† 'is a necessary one and a short cut is educationally unsound. The student's need is rather of help in tolerating her own discomfort, perhaps for quite a long time'. The third function of the supervisor, then, is to distinguish between the differing needs of individuals. Some may need more direct advice than others – not necessarily because of less competence – and it is no good having one pet line of approach for all. This particularly needs to be said to the non-directive as well as to the directive supervisor, for it is so easy to take the line 'how much better for them to make their own decisions' and to forget that the capacity to take responsibility, like any other, has to grow.‡ Anxiety and insecurity may be increased if an uncertain student feels he has been left unhelped, floundering in a bog. At the same time, I think it is fair to say that tutors more commonly err in giving too much direction than in giving too little.

This leads on to another point, implicit in the quotation from Ashdown and Brown. The supervisor provides steadying support when things are not going well, as much as or more than when they are. Of all the functions of the supervisor, this is one of the most essential and the most difficult to fulfil in practice:§ in fact it could be said that this is the acid test of the quality of the supervision. It is so easy to undermine confidence

* 'Learning that changes behaviour substantially is most likely to result when a person himself tries to improve a situation that makes a difference to him' (Corey, 1953, p. 9).

† Ashdown & Brown (1953, p. 100).

‡ A special difficulty here concerns mistakes and errors that may damage third parties – children in school, clients of the trainee social worker, and so on. Spoiled materials are the natural risk of learning by doing, in cooking, wood-carving, or art, but they cannot be tolerated where living subjects are concerned. It is clearly the supervisor's responsibility to prevent that stage being reached and I am certain that he *must* step in decisively here.

§ In Whyte's paradox, 'One of the most difficult things for a supervisor to do is not to supervise' (1957, p. 225).

when making criticisms that *have* to be made, and to allow an element of personal blame to creep in. A training college lecturer was describing an interview with an unsatisfactory student: 'I went through the lesson with Miss Exe and showed her where it was wrong – she didn't seem at all interested (see note 1 below). So then I said, "I suppose you're spending a lot of time on the affairs of the Union because you're certainly not spending it on your work", but I couldn't get her to admit anything (see note 2). She's got no contact with the children at all – they don't bother to play her up but just go their own way and leave her alone (note 3). And then to my amazement she said, "Anyway I know I can teach, and I know the children like me" (note 4). So I said, "They don't, they hate you and won't have anything to do with you" ' (note 5).

[1] The usual defence against criticism.
[2] The implicit notion is of a prisoner before a judge.
[3] An important and acute observation.   [4] Defence by counter-assertion.
[5] Unforgivable, particularly so in view of the insight in note 3.

This is the last way in which a student who lacks contact should be handled. It would be worth while asking what contact that supervisor had with the student – it is to be hoped that she had none, for otherwise the effect of her remarks could not be anything except damaging.

Although this was a young student (the twenty years' difference between the ages of supervisor and student did not, one fears, involve a twenty years' difference in maturity) and although it was particularly bad supervision, this example puts in focus what is a temptation to us all – to panic when we see really bad errors being made and to feel that we *must* ram in our righteous indignation. But ramming in does not help – it is likely to arouse defensiveness and to increase insecurity. The first aim should be to find out whether the student is *aware* that things are going wrong. In the example given, Miss Exe was apparently oblivious of any shortcomings, but one cannot be sure of this because the supervisor did everything possible to make defensiveness inevitable, whereas the prime need is to get a clear picture of what the student – the person mainly concerned – thinks of the situation. Older students at least are usually only too aware of the difficulties, and it is most desirable to give them an opportunity to state the position as they see it, before we rush in with our comments. This has several advantages: (a) it avoids appearing to blame; (b) difficulties that are admitted are then common ground and open to discussion, unlike the battle over every point in the example; (c) explanation may show that some of the difficulties are not of the student's making, and so there is no risk of mistaken criticism and injured innocence; (d) it is possible to find out if it has been a bad day and so not a fair sample of what usually occurs; (e) it gives the tutor an opportunity of seeing how much insight the student has (and is the *only* way of discovering the rare case of the student who does not show any realization that anything is amiss, for once defensiveness has been aroused one can never tell); (f) above all, it establishes that the supervisor is on the student's side. This is crucial: as long as the student feels that the tutor is hostile, there will be resentment, even in the face of carefully just and temperate criticism; whereas the feeling that the supervisor sees the difficulties yet remains on the student's side makes the latter more ready to accept (not just to swallow) any necessary criticism. The familiar childhood story of the wager between sun and wind as to who would remove a man's overcoat is apposite here: the harder the wind blew, the more tightly the man pulled his coat round him, but it came off in the warm sun. Batterings from outside do not overcome defences, they make them more necessary; and the supervisor who says 'This is bad' is merely making it harder, not easier, for the 'badness' to be dealt with *effectively*. The best rule to take is that most students are as worried as the supervisor, or more so, and anything that savours of personal blame is right off the mark.

Support and acceptance, however, do not mean that the supervisor minimizes the difficulties – such an attitude would signify to the student that he was not understood, that his efforts were belittled, and that he was not being treated with candour – with the effect of increasing suspicion and insecurity. 'Don't worry', when you can't help worrying; 'everything is lovely', when you know perfectly well it isn't – these are infuriating and subtly insulting remarks. More support, oddly enough, is given to the depressed student by accepting the reality of his discouragement than by jollying him along with statements such as 'It will all come right in the end'. It is better to face with him the present fact that he feels badly about things than to try to gloss it over. On one occasion a tutor was asked by a third party to have a word with a particularly unapproachable student, a middle-aged man who had set himself very high standards and was disappointed that the reality of his work did not come up to his expectations. After considerable fencing, the supervisor managed to elicit this, and thereafter rang the changes with him on 'How disappointed you must feel' and 'You weren't expecting things to be like this', until finally it seemed safe to insert 'Possibly you were expecting too much too quickly', which led to the student's eventual comment 'It might be better if I climbed down a bit'. I do not believe that direct reassurance, telling him how good his work really was, would have met the situation as adequately as did the willingness to accept his discouragement; or that short-circuiting, by beginning with an interpretation, however justified, on the lines, 'Now I think you're expecting too much . . .', would have had much effect. On the operative level, it is not what the tutor thinks, but what the student is prepared to accept, that counts.

This same comment holds in the rare case when a student (let us call him Mr. Wye) is genuinely unaware that his work is unsatisfactory. Unless Mr. Wye can be brought to realize this, he will feel himself unjustly treated; and to help him to realize it, it is not enough simply to tell him so, still less to keep bludgeoning it at him, which he will rightly interpret as a personal attack, as in the example of the young student Miss Exe. How best to bring it home to him will vary according to the circumstances, but an essential prerequisite is to avoid any element of personal condemnation. When Mr. Wye finally said 'You've been very sympathetic to me', at the close of an interview during which he had received a severe shock to his complacency, he was in fact paying his supervisor a considerable tribute. It may sometimes be necessary, as on this occasion, for a supervisor to be very blunt in his criticisms, but this should not obscure, even in the extreme case, that supervisor and student are on the same side of the battlements.

We have seen that students vary considerably in the level at which they are functioning and also that the provision of acceptance and support is an important element in supervision. It follows, then, that a dead level of efficiency, still less of perfection, can never be a legitimate goal, but that the supervisor should be prepared for inescapably various ends. To tolerate something which is less than the best, as he sees it, is not easy; but to screw all to the same level of endeavour is doomed to failure. For a student who is at stage A, it may be real progress to move to B and C, and to expect him to be at D and E is to expect the impossible, irrespective of where others may be. It is said that the best can be the enemy of the good, and it may be that to put forward an ideal which is impossible of realization *in a particular case* is to prevent consolidation on a lower, more realistic, and (for this man) more valuable level. Several examples may make the point at issue clearer. To teach a class efficiently involves skills which have to be learned. Having acquired these skills, a young teacher may be able to work with groups and later with individuals, but 'individual teaching' as an initial goal is too ambitious. Again, it is rightly said that 'free methods' make heavy demands on the teacher's skill – where, then, is the sense in *requiring* them of every teacher? Surely it would be wiser to wait and encourage growth. Similarly, self-discipline no doubt is the only true discipline, but it is too much to expect of immature children. A probation officer who exhorts may not be the best kind of probation officer, but within his limits he can do useful work.

What I am pleading for is the recognition of stages in the development and growth of skill, so that we do not try to make people run before they can walk, and so that each learns at his own level and is encouraged to move forward at his own pace. The watchword is consolidation, and a slow consolidated advance is more valuable than hothouse forcing. In the parable of the sower, the seeds which came up too quickly from shallow soil soon withered and died. In the long run, none of us can go against our natural bent: we have a preferred tempo, a preferred style of living. I have no doubt that there are some teachers and probation officers who are happier and more effective instructing and exhorting than they would be if they were using methods which are 'better' – for others, though not for them – and it seems rather odd if in the name of 'freedom' they are to be coerced. It is not a contradiction in terms if a dictatorial headmaster lays down the law to his assistants as to what methods they shall adopt, but it is if a 'progressive' one does so – and the same holds good of supervisors and students. My contention is that in the last analysis more is gained by acceptance of the imperfect than by pressing for something for which the student is not yet ready (and for which he may never be ready). Perhaps, later, he may feel able to take one step farther on and, when that has been similarly consolidated, another: but all the time keeping within his depth. 'The educatee is a person, not a thing to be educated in the fixed beliefs of the educator or in the fashion of the day' (F.S.).

So far, reference has been made to supervision as a means of helping. For many courses, especially those of a professional nature, this is not the whole of the story, and it is inescapable that the 'assessment' side of supervision should be to some extent at variance with what has been said, particularly in the last few paragraphs. It must be admitted that 'acceptance' and 'tolerance' cannot be unlimited when academic and professional qualifications are at stake, and this simple fact alone may seem to make valueless the emphasis placed on personal security. The question will be taken up in more detail in the next chapter, but here it is important to say emphatically that where the supervisor of practical work is also an assessor for examination purposes he has a duty not only to the student but also to the maintenance of the standard of the qualification. A very weak student can be helped along the lines suggested, but it may also be necessary to fail him. It does not seem to me that this involves a contradiction, although undeniably it complicates the issue and makes it more difficult to establish a good working relationship.*

The assessment of practical work can be dealt with briefly. It is only fair that reasonable allowance should be made for particularly difficult conditions outside the student's control, and also that undue credit should not be given to a student working in good conditions. The amount of effort put forth and the direction and extent of change (for example, a student who started off very weak but is rapidly improving) can also be considered, but not overweighted – the main thing is not to moralize, but to consider the general level. Window-dressing needs to be watched for, and discounted. At the same time, the less tangible indicants have to be taken into account. Standards should be kept as steady as possible among different candidates – no easy matter in practice when circumstances vary widely. Chance fluctuations – the good day or the bad day – should be minimized. My own feeling is that there is little value in trying to be too precise; the important thing is to be careful at those borderlines which really matter (of failure, for example)

* The apparent contradiction comes from a confusion between 'accepting' and 'passing', and can be resolved if these terms are kept clear; thus Mr. Wye felt himself accepted although he had been told he was unlikely to pass. It is the immature supervisor who causes the confusion by rejecting and blaming (personally) those who are likely to fail (e.g. Miss Exe); presumably this supervisor considered it a credit to herself if her students did well and a personal affront if they did not.

and not to argue the toss between B- and B. There is no place for sympathy or disapproval. In sum, the attempt is to be as objective as possible, and the assessment should not only be fair, but also appear so.

In these pages I have dealt with practical work almost entirely from the point of view of the supervising tutor. In closing, I should like to summarize the implications of this chapter for the student.

1. 'Where you are' is what matters. Practical work must of necessity start from this.
2. Objectives can be tailor-made to fit the individual, if the organization of the course is flexible enough.
3. There is no case for the imposition of identical requirements.
4. The only partial exception comes when a standard of qualification is demanded.
5. There should be a tolerance of wide variations in methods and approach, once the irreducible minimum has been achieved.
6. Students learn something from hearing lecturers talk, more from talking themselves, most of all from what they actually do.
7. The most favourable conditions are when students can reflect on what they are doing and feel sufficiently free to regard their supervisors as consultants, not as judges.
8. The least favourable conditions are when anxiety, self-consciousness, and the rigid imposition of external requirements clamp their energies into a narrow mould.
9. Consolidation is essential.

Chapter Six

EXAMINATIONS

IT IS very easy, particularly for those in universities and similar establishments where examinations are part of the accepted order, to take them for granted and apply them as a matter of course, whether the subjects be young students or adults. On the other hand, it is not enough just to say dogmatically that adults should not be faced with the strain of examinations. Further consideration is required as to what *is* the effect of examinations on older persons, and particularly whether any alternative schemes would be likely to be any *better* in averting tension and anxiety.

We are not concerned, then, with the accuracy or inaccuracy of examinations as measuring instruments,* which has been the usual target of criticism, but with their subjective concomitants, which have been surprisingly little studied. In what follows I shall draw heavily on an investigation I made some years ago into the reactions of adult students to examinations, with the above questions in mind. The results of that investigation were reported in the *British Journal of Educational Psychology*† and can be briefly summarized as follows. A number of my former students sent replies to a short questionnaire. The majority felt that a written examination was necessary; that its abolition would

* For a discussion of this, reference should be made to Valentine (1932, 1938), Hartog & Rhodes (1935), and Hartog, Rhodes & Burt (1942).

† February 1956. I am grateful to the Editor, Prof. P. E. Vernon, for permission to use material from that article.

adversely affect the status of their qualification; and that it was less upsetting than the practical test (of teaching handicapped children) which also formed part of the requirements of London University. No significant differences of sex and age were found, but men and younger persons tended to be more opposed to written examinations than women and older persons. There appeared to be no relation between differences in type of teacher-training, in academic ability, or in teaching proficiency, and favourable or unfavourable opinions regarding examinations.

Those who are interested in the numerical results, analysed into categories, and in the precautions taken to ensure that the sample was representative and the findings accurate, may be referred for further details to the article; but I emphasize here that I believe that considerable care was, in fact, taken and that the replies do represent the honest, conscious opinion of the writers. Although it is an inescapable characteristic of the questionnaire method that it is confined to opinions which are consciously held, the possibility that rationalization may occasionally have occurred should not lead us to reject the material out of hand, but only to remember its limitations.

What seems to me of general interest and importance is the light which the replies throw on individual differences among adult students in attitude and in the extent and sources of anxiety; I shall accordingly discuss them in detail, taking the questions in turn and quoting freely from the replies.

To the first question: 'Do you think that an examination is a fair means of assessing the work done during the year?' 64 answered 'Yes' and 15 'No'. The large majority in favour is perhaps rather surprising, but it was by no means an uncritical or inarticulate majority. The general opinion seemed to be that an examination performs a useful and necessary function and that it is reasonably fair in its operation, provided certain safe-guards are maintained. This blanket statement can be split up into its constituent parts.

The usefulness of examinations was said by some to lie in providing a focus for effort. Several said that they were stimulated to work for a clearly defined goal; others considered that their studies were too closely organized by the examination goal to be beneficial; one went so far as to suggest that people did the minimum to cover the syllabus, clearly implying that more would have been done had this artificial restriction been removed. The function of setting a standard was also frequently mentioned, but again there was an occasional dissentient voice, one asserting that examinations were redundant, because the standard either had or had not been reached at the end of the course. This writer did not go on to consider what is surely the main difficulty of his viewpoint, that it is difficult to convince someone that he has not reached the standard without leaving him with a feeling of injustice. But this omission was abundantly rectified by others who pointed out that examinations provide a safeguard both for the candidate and for the tutor, since an external examiner reads all the papers. Thus the impersonality of an examination, which is resented by some, is considered by others a point in its favour. Several mentioned that they were thrown back on their own knowledge and were forced to clarify their minds.

Further comments about the function of examinations were that they provide a salutary discipline (one feels that one would like to examine more closely the unconscious assumptions here); that they keep one down to earth; that they provide an all-round view of the knowledge of the candidate and can throw at least an indirect light on his probable practical competence; and that they provide evidence as to the degree to which the course is fulfilling its purpose. This last is an interesting point, to which other comments bear witness. Two writers suggested that the gains or losses of a course can be assessed only over a period of time, and others that an examination cannot be expected to reveal independent thought and is of necessity superficial. One man summed up the issues here with clarity

95

and asperity: 'Only the years will prove if you are, in fact, producing thoughtful, positive, and constructive teachers; only the years will tell if you have taught them to think for themselves. In the meantime the written examination will at least tell you that they have, or have not, absorbed what they have been told during the year. Whether they have been critical or not, whether they have worked it into the pattern of their own experience, or whether they are going to trot it out like so many puppets, is a thing you will find out later, but the examination does at least do one thing – it eliminates those who are unable even to absorb the year's work.'

We pass now to the question of fairness. Surprisingly, very few commented adversely on the element of chance in the appearance of questions on a paper; others mentioned that the effect of luck was minimized provided a wide enough range was covered. It is heartening, if hardly relevant, that several (not all good candidates) considered their examination 'easy' – at any rate it suggests contentment on the issue of fairness. (Examiners who read this may be amused to know that one reply suggested that the art in framing questions is to make them appear difficult and therefore impressive to the uninitiated, whereas the candidates recognize that they are really easy!) A few spoke of being 'not good on paper' or 'unable to express myself'; another, who claimed to be equally non-verbal, stated that, whereas he would expect to be handicapped in writing a literary essay, he found that as long as the questions related to work within his practical experience he could answer without undue difficulty. Others believed that on the whole things tended to average out. A common complaint was that older people may become rusty and may have greater difficulty in marshalling their thoughts quickly, and some mentioned the time factor in an examination as a definite bugbear. The question of illness was also raised: three mentioned that they sat the examination suffering from more or less severe illness; and a large number spoke of inconvenient physical conditions –

excessive sleepiness and fatigue, stomach ache, cramp not only of the hand but of the whole body through maintaining the same position for long periods, hard chairs, and the like. Some at least of these are more likely to be an acute source of discomfort to older people than to children and adolescents. It must be remembered, too, that a digestive disorder can be 'minor' from a medical point of view and still be a considerable handicap at the time. It is interesting that of the four replies received from teachers who had not passed the examination, none used this particular line, though three of them considered that it did not provide a fair estimate (the remaining one did); two of these mentioned events prior to the examination as having had an unsettling effect. The issue of fairness was most searchingly examined in one contribution, from which I now quote at length.

'Clearly the examining body has a right to ensure that the candidate is a fit person to hold a diploma. In my view, a properly constructed examination on the work of the year is not the least valuable means of doing so, for it has the merit in most cases of giving the examiners a fairly clear "all-round view". Nor should it be forgotten that such an examination can have another very proper purpose – that of indicating how effectively the course is realizing its purpose. Reference was made earlier to "a properly constructed examination". By that I meant – speaking as a layman – that the examination should be:

'(a) Relevant – it should in fact examine what it is meant to examine.
'(b) Lucid – the questions should leave the candidate in no doubt as to what is required of him.
'(c) Authoritative – this is hard to define, but I mean that the candidate should gain the impression that he is being examined by people who "know their job". A wartime friend of mine had studied conscientiously to qualify as a gunnery

97

instructor. He failed his final examination. When I sympathized with him he said, "I'm disappointed, but I've no complaints. It was a fair examination. Those chaps certainly know their job."

'(d) Comfortable – that is, all reasonable steps should be taken to put the candidates at ease.'

Few people were prepared to stand or fall solely on the result of their written papers, but the majority considered them fair, provided certain safeguards were maintained. These usually took the form of a stipulation that 'reasonable credit' should be given for the year's work, and that 'reasonable allowance' should be made for known difficulties. These points were made more frequently than any other single ones and may be taken as generally agreed. Several seemed to take it for granted that such conditions had in fact been fulfilled – as one woman put it, 'No internal examiner is going to allow a good candidate to fail because of one bad paper'. Furthermore, it was pointed out that many teachers tend to expect too much of themselves and that it might even be a relief to them to have an outside judgement, which was likely to be more balanced and less strict than their own.

To the second question: 'Were you conscious of feeling unduly tense as the examination date approached or during the examination?' 34 answered 'Yes' and 45 'No'.

To the third question: 'Did your close associates (husband, wife, children, parents) find you difficult just before or during the examination?' 17 answered 'Yes' and 62 'No'.

These questions can conveniently be discussed together. Tension and strain constitute one of the most objectionable features of examinations and provide a ready target for criticism, so opinion on this point may be particularly valuable. At the same time, one must concede that certain personalities may need to deny the existence of disrupting emotions, and this may falsify the reported results to an unknown extent. Even so, it is perhaps surprising that the majority should have answered 'No' to the second question. The key-word, of course, is 'unduly', and this was deliberately left undefined. Some degree of nervousness is to be expected before an important occasion; it is only when it threatens to get out of hand that it may constitute an unfair handicap. However, it was just on this point, as to whether or not it is a handicap, that there were sharp differences of opinion. By no means all of the 34 who admitted to feeling keyed up considered that this affected their performance adversely; the majority thought that it did not. There were numerous comments to the effect that once they started the examination they were all right, and one candidate considered that she was helped to do her best work by being strung up. In sharp contrast is the blank misery of those four (all of whom passed) who were persistently plagued by nerves; and a case might be put forward that what the majority suffer or do not suffer is in this matter irrelevant and that, if even a small minority are handicapped, this in itself is the gravamen of the charge against examinations. It is possible to argue for or against the statement that adults should be able to exercise self-control: some may consider it unduly smug, but if it is made by those who are themselves highly strung and who have reached this self-control only with difficulty, who is to say that their difficulties are greater or less than those of others who did not control their nerves? As one woman put it: 'I think this is a case where it is easy to criticize but not so easy to be constructive. I doubt if anyone really enjoys the prospect of a written examination, but the question is not quite the same for an adult as for a child. Children can, in a few cases, do themselves serious injustice because of "nerves" at the time, but my personal feeling is that an adult should have sufficient control and maturity to face the situation and produce something within measurable distance of his best. I would say that what one gains on the swings one loses on the roundabouts. One may suffer from examination nerves and be strong on English, or vice versa. There may be an odd lucky candidate and an odd unlucky one – which brings up another big question: after all, if one cannot control one's nerves and if English is a weak point, isn't it perhaps just that the pass mark is not reached?'

Several asserted that nervousness might in some cases be related to lack of knowledge, and that it could best be allayed beforehand by adequate preparation. Although one can readily assent to the statement as it stands, it does not follow that the converse is also true. Others suggested that wide outside interests were a good insurance against undue tension. The question of age was raised, and opinion was equally divided between those who considered older people more, and those who considered them less, liable to be upset than children and adolescents. Frequent mention was made of the heavy responsibility felt by students towards the Local Education Authority which had sent them to take the course; and there were also difficulties concerning financial worries and family responsibilities – all of which bear hard on mature students and tend to increase the tension. One woman suggested that a line of demarcation, as regards feelings of responsibility, could be drawn between all adults on the one hand, and adolescent students on the other, not between older and younger adults – the youngest members of our group* would be more different from 18-year-olds than they were from their older colleagues. Another pointed out that adults who had heavy home responsibilities might find that these adversely affected their work during the course, but in an examination they were in the same position as the other candidates and their confidence was restored.

The important group of four who did not pass the written examination should be considered separately. Because the numbers are so small, to avoid any possibility of identification, detailed statements of individuals will not be given. In general, their comments could have been parallelled from the larger

---

* Ages at the time of taking the examination ranged from 27 to 51 years.

group, and they did not stand out as being *exceptionally* handicapped by nerves, though all answered 'Yes' to the second question. Indeed, one said that when he actually started to write his fears vanished and he wrote fluently and easily. What is more serious is the long-term effect of failure in an examination on the confidence of the individual concerned. This was mentioned, and fully documented, by two out of the four: even though they are doing good work in their respective schools, the wound has not healed. It may be thought that this is a heavy charge against examinations, but in all fairness it must be remembered that, whatever the mode of assessment, any result that separates some from the rest is bound to be felt as a blemish by the individuals concerned. It may even be that failure in an examination, which provides convenient scapegoats such as nerves, unlucky questions, and so on, is easier to bear than a total setback such as failure on overall assessment.

Turning now to the third question, it is interesting to note that considerably fewer of those who admitted to feeling tense said that it affected their associates. Most of them believed that their nervousness was known to themselves alone – they 'bottled up their feelings' or 'adopted an air of bravado' – but at the same time they spoke of the understanding and help they received from members of their families, and it is probable that the number of those who were difficult at home is an under-estimate.

A final point of some importance which was brought out in a number of replies was the existence of strain throughout the course, not confined to the examination period only, though that may well have been the last straw. One man, however, said that tension was less at the time of the examination than earlier on. It would certainly be optimistic to imagine that if we got rid of examinations all tension would immediately vanish.

This provides a convenient transition to a discussion of the fourth question: 'Can you suggest any alternative form of assessment of the year's work?' In this section many respondents gave no suggestions but those that were given were often highly individual and worked out in considerable detail.

Numerically, the commonest suggestion was that all work done during the course should be assessed. Various methods of weighting were put forward, which distinguish this suggestion from the one discussed earlier of allowing 'reasonable credit' without laying down precise conditions. Others explicitly rejected this proposal on the ground that, though it would spread strain more evenly through the year, it would not diminish the total amount, and indeed would be more likely to increase it, since every error would 'count'. There would be a waste of effort in putting *all* work into 'presentable' form. Further, it would handicap those who were improving all the time. It is probable that, on reflection, others, in addition to those who expressed their disapproval, would find it an extremely unalluring prospect; it may be a case where the remedy could easily prove worse than the disease. Not all of those who put forward the suggestion considered it a substitute for a written examination: some regarded it as a supplement.

A thesis, in one form or another, was another proposal. One stipulated that to be valuable it should be very closely linked to practical work in school, and that a purely bookish thesis should not be accepted; another suggested a 'thesis under examination conditions'; the remainder who advocated a thesis contented themselves with urging that it should be of a really high standard since only then would it be generally accepted as an equivalent to a written examination. Not all of the supporters of a thesis were anti-examination: one proposed the thesis as a supplement; another suggested that individuals could choose between taking an examination and producing a high quality thesis based on original work, a thesis which could be accepted as a contribution to its subject. How many theses would appear under those conditions was not stated. The advantages of the thesis were put forward as follows: 'Such a work gives opportunity, without distressing conditions, for students to demonstrate the originality and quality of their thoughts; their industry and interest; and the effect upon them of their training. And these are real valuations in which the examiners are presumably interested.' The thesis, however, had its critics. One said that it would simply substitute a long worry for a short one; another, that the average person would find it much more exacting, since original thinkers were few and far between. Two suggested that it might have a very narrowing effect – 'I do not feel that a thesis would be a suitable alternative. In a choice of subject I should naturally try to avoid just those very aspects of the work in which I most needed detailed knowledge, and concentrate on those with which I already felt myself most at home. This could not be done even with the fairly wide choice of questions in the examination, and consequently I left the Institute knowing considerably more of the organization and conduct of E.S.N.* schools, of after-care, and general provision for handicapped children, than I should ever have taken the trouble to make part of myself without the felt need to have it ready for examination day.'

The remaining suggestions were all put forward singly. One woman said that a prepared essay using all available reference material and handed in strictly on a given date would go far to meet the critics, if used in conjunction with the usual type of examination. Another interesting but difficult suggestion was this: 'An additional (not alternative) form of assessment might be provided by giving, in examination conditions, each candidate a paper or pamphlet on some aspect of the year's work. It would be controversial, of course, and the examinee would be required to give a critical analysis of the facts and opinions expressed therein. It could even contain a deliberate mistake! . . . This would give information about the examinee's ability to deal critically with printed matter, and should give a useful indication of whether or not he can use any ideas absorbed

* Educationally sub-normal.

during his year's work as a measure for assessing the validity of other opinions. It might go a little deeper than the straight answer to a reasonably straight question in the usual written examination. In other words, he might more clearly reveal what he has taken out of his year's work and made a part of himself, for examinees do tend to write what they feel will be acceptable to the examiners, quoting wherever possible the examiners' own words.'

One advocated regular tests with prepared material; another proposed that a monthly report of his work should be given to each student; a third suggested that since the single word 'Pass' might blanket a whole range of differences from unusually good to a bare scrape, classes should be awarded as in degree examinations; a fourth asked for mock finals. These four suggestions, whatever their merits or demerits, have in common that they extend rather than narrow the range of examinable material.

Finally, a miscellany. The test of practical competence should be more heavily weighted than the written papers; it should be possible to credit a good practical performance against weak theory (but not vice versa); the written papers should consist of a lot of short questions; they should consist of only one or two long questions; there should be an oral examination for those who do not do themselves justice on paper; the test should be 'How much has he given to the course, not what has he got out of it' (but how is this to be assessed, one wonders).

To sum up this section, the general opinion on the value of examinations seemed to be 'improve but do not discard them'. Whether the suggested improvements would in fact be improvements, or whether in the eyes of some iconoclasts they might appear unduly conservative if not retrograde, need not be discussed here.

The fifth question: 'Do you think that the absence of a final examination would affect the status of the diploma?' brought the following replies: 62 'Yes', 11 'No', and 6 'Unable to judge.'

Of all the questions, this provoked the most dogmatic statements. It should be noted that the opinions people expressed were not necessarily their own, but what they believed to be those most commonly held by others. Several expressed regret: 'Unfortunately, yes', or 'In the present state of educational opinion, yes', or referred to a future time of presumably greater enlightenment. Others aligned themselves firmly with what they stated to be the generally held opinion – that by examination and examination only was there a 'real' test of one's worth. The number of assumptions is perhaps instructive here: more than half simply took it for granted that in the absence of written papers the diploma would be given to all candidates indiscriminately. What is more, those who did not think this themselves asserted that their colleagues would think so and would need a lot of persuading to the contrary. Statements like these abounded: 'I am not certain here, but I lean to the view that outsiders prefer a diploma to be "earned" by examination, and tend to value such an award more highly than a diploma automatically presented for attending the course.' 'I think there is a widespread belief that examination results do provide a measure of competence and, however misguided this view may be, I feel it exists and should be considered.' 'May I say frankly that I feel that this suggested abolition of the written examination smacks too much of the modern tendency to make life so easy that initiative is sapped and the healthy personal striving to overcome difficulties is quite stultified.' Surprisingly, the Emergency Training Scheme was mentioned only twice, once to say that its success afforded clear indication that written papers were not necessary, and the second time in a contrary sense. One man said that he had changed his mind with the lapse of time: immediately after he sat the examination, he would have considered it unnecessary, but now he felt it necessary 'to maintain standards'. Another suggested that it would be well to suspect rationalizations of an inverted 'sour-grapes' type – since I have had to go through this ordeal, I will agitate that everyone else shall have to go through it too, before reaching the grapes!

The most serious arguments ranged round the possibility of maintaining a standard in the absence of an examination: the majority thought that this could not be done, or at least that it would be impossible to convince others that it had been maintained; a small minority considered that it could be done on condition that it was generally known that the diploma was not automatically awarded, becoming in effect a certificate of attendance. This is the real issue, but even here no one attempted to explain how it was to become 'generally known'.

It seems reasonable to conclude that the root of the matter is to be found in the question of withholding or not withholding an award, and that the precise form the assessment takes is of secondary importance and can be governed mainly by considerations of convenience, ease of administration, and demonstrable fairness. Manifestations of tension, such as were described in the previous section, are a regrettable but inescapable adjunct, not merely of written papers, but of any form of assessment which results in the giving or withholding of an award. The point is that success is not certain and hence tension results. But if success *were* to be certain, its value would largely disappear. I take it that this is the real meaning of the overwhelming majority who answered 'Yes' to this question.

To the sixth question: 'Did you feel that the written examination was more or less upsetting than the practical one, or did you not notice any difference?' the replies were as follows: 17 thought the written examination worse, 42 thought the practical examination worse; the remaining 20 said 'They were so different that they cannot be compared', or 'Both were about the same', or 'Neither was in the slightest degree upsetting.'

This question was included on the assumption (which turned out to be very wide of the mark) that there would be a great outcry against the examination, and I wanted to check whether the target of criticism was genuinely the written papers or whether it was any situation in which people felt themselves judged. However, although the assumption was mistaken, the question turned out to be very worth while.

Representative replies are as follows: 'The practical one was far more upsetting than the written one. In spite of my age and experience, I cannot yet do my best in face of authority. I get nervous, het up, and have an extreme feeling of inferiority when I know I am being watched. The written examination gives one time to collect one's thoughts and compose oneself.' 'I found the written examination easier than the practical, inasmuch as we knew more definitely the work to be done and it could be done "solo".' 'I found the written examination more upsetting than the practical one, because I thought more depended on it. In any case, I did not know the practical examination was taking place when it did! I considered it a routine supervision. However, I dislike teaching with anyone else in the room, always – a weakness, perhaps, which I have found common to many other teachers.' 'I was very happy during my practical work and I can imagine others being less fortunate in their school placing, but I can honestly say that I found the written examination *less* upsetting than the practical one.'

On the whole, the practical work (which lasted for eight weeks) was felt as a greater strain, mainly because it was more prolonged, whereas the written papers were a 'short, sharp shock', but soon over. (It is worth bearing this point in mind in connection with schemes that assess all work done in the course.) Two mentioned the uncertainty of the date of the practical test as an additional source of anxiety; again, this can be contrasted with the usual view of the undesirable building-up of tension as a known examination date draws inexorably nearer. It probably means that those who are apprehensive will be so, whatever the attendant circumstances. On the other hand, there was some evidence to suggest that attempts to reduce tension can have some effect: 'After careful consideration I still cannot see that the examination puts the candidate to any disadvantage. It is not unreasonable to test him on the work he contracted to do by virtue of entering upon the course – and that is all the examination does. Further, I repeat my belief that, throughout, his best interests are carefully – if not anxiously – protected.' Or, conversely: 'I felt at times as though I were on trial, if not for my life, at least for my living and for my intelligence. We all accept the fact that children must feel accepted and secure to do their best. I rarely felt either.' The same efforts which appease some disturb others, and the personalities of the supervisors were commented on, favourably or unfavourably, by several. To avoid undue subjectivity of judgement, one woman suggested that all students, not merely some as at present, should be assessed by an external examiner in practical teaching. The reactivation of earlier attitudes was mentioned by a man who said that he felt himself thrown back to his final teaching practice as a training-college student, and by a woman who said that after a number of years of successful teaching she found herself resenting being again in the position of a student; and no doubt this would be true, too, of a number of others. It was stated several times that it was impossible to equalize conditions over a number of different schools and, even though allowance was made for differing circumstances in assessing candidates, this was felt to be a drawback of the practical test as compared with the written papers, which were the same for all.

An interesting conflict of opinion came up over the question of self-consciousness. Some mentioned that the presence of the children in the practical test was a help to them in forgetting themselves in what they were doing, whereas in the written papers there was no escape from themselves; on the other hand, others spoke of greater self-consciousness during the practical test, and to some of these it was a source of self-annoyance, for they felt that as seasoned campaigners they 'ought' to have been unruffled. Furthermore, the children provided an element of independent variation. 'All this worried me because I felt

that it was the "teaching" that was to be inspected by the supervisor and I couldn't begin to teach until I had the cooperation of the children and the right atmosphere in the classroom.'
'In the practical examination, even the most meticulous preparation and arrangement could be upset by a change in the school routine – medical inspection, prize days, open days, absences, lack or change of accommodation, etc., and more often than not such changes occurred on the morning that the examiner arrived at the school.'

Finally, there was a miscellaneous group of comments which tended to cancel each other out. Suggestions for improvement included: a longer time in school; a shorter time in school; no time at all in school; school work to be split into two shorter sections; a heavier weighting to be given to practical performance; assessment in one's own school the following year in place of a practical test; and removal of the period spent in school from the proximity of the written examination, by putting either the practical work or the written papers earlier.

To sum up, the variety of impressions, reactions, and recommendations is somewhat bewildering, but at least it is safe to say that the written papers are not the only, and perhaps not even the chief, villain of the piece.

The seventh question was, 'Any other comments?' This proved a useful addendum, and produced a wide range of comments and criticisms on all aspects of the course, as well as on the examination itself. Many of them are not relevant to the present issue, but it is worth while gathering together the remaining pertinent points, which may be of general, as opposed to purely domestic, interest.

The concentration which then existed (it was changed as a result of this investigation) of four three-hour papers into two days was strongly criticized and a plea was put forward for spreading them, to avoid undue fatigue. No mention was made of revision between the papers and this does not seem to have been a motive in advocating the change.

Habits of work came out by implication. One said that she had been cured of last-minute revision by thoroughly muddling herself as an adolescent; several that they had stopped work some days before the examination; one woman strongly criticized the week of revision prior to the examination; but, apart from these, no mention was made of revision, and I have no reason to suppose that last-minute cramming constituted any difficulty. (The word 'cramming' was not mentioned by anyone throughout.)

It was suggested by one that the methods of assessment should be explained to the students, and by another that all students should be informed of their progress. This type of comment is useful, in that it underlines the difference between points of view and shows that what seems obvious in one frame of reference is not equally obvious at the receiving end. One always tends to take for granted that procedures are equally clear to all concerned, but this may not be so.

Finally, with regard to the examination itself, bad lighting, the glare from dead-white paper, and papers which were harder/easier than those in previous/successive years, were all mentioned – but surely not even the most intro-punitive examiner will accept responsibility for a heat-wave.

The essential point that emerges from the investigation, it seems to me, is the question as to whether a qualification should be awarded automatically. There is general agreement that this is undesirable, and, even if the price to be paid is uncertainty and tension, some degree of these must be accepted as inevitable (though every effort should be made to get rid of *undue* tension). To me the question of examinations is rather a side issue; the important one is the maintenance of standards (by whatever procedure of assessment appears most convenient), and as a recent student said tersely, 'Minimum standards there clearly must be'. No one wants to fail, but I think that adults still less want to feel that they have gained a qualification without deserving it, and which, therefore, they cannot respect.

Chapter Seven

AUTHORITY

THE EARLIER chapters of this book have dealt mainly with matters concerning the group as a whole; however, the chapter on supervision touched on some questions of personal relationships which must now be examined more closely. When one turns to matters relating to individuals, a dilemma at once arises – where and how is the question of authority to be dealt with? It was very tempting to give this chapter a non-committal title such as 'Interaction', in the hope that this might play down what would otherwise appear to be an unjustified emphasis on one part only of a more inclusive whole. But difficulties do not vanish just by labelling, and it is common experience that when one individual has power, in however indirect and diluted a form, over another, the fact is not readily overlooked but tends to colour the subsequent exchanges between them. There is, then, something to be said for dealing with this aspect first and openly, and getting it out of the way, as long as it is not suggested that the power element is the only, or the most important, consideration.

We are all people; and that common experience is far more important than the accidents or capacities that stratify us along lines of class, nation, or official position – a truism, but one that needs continual repetition, since there are so many temptations to forget it. Of these temptations, those connected with the existence of hierarchies of power* are among the most damaging, not only in their effect on the leaders (on the lines of Lord Acton's famous dictum 'Power tends to corrupt, and absolute power corrupts absolutely'), but as much if not more in their effect on the led. A leader, for instance, may genuinely wish to adopt a man-to-man approach; he may think he has succeeded; but the chances are that his subordinates will not forget his position even if he appears to have done so. Unless this is stated plainly, it will stultify the approach adopted in Chapter 5 and make it sound unrealistic: it is not enough for the supervisor to have good intentions, and to 'wish to help', in order for everything to be plain sailing.

The tutor, then, should keep in mind the following statements, unpalatable though some of them may be:

1. It is no good wishing the authority problem out of existence. He will have to come to terms with it.
2. He is a sitting target for any previously formed attitudes to authority. They will be projected on to him whether or not he deserves them.
3. Nevertheless, his conduct can modify or entrench such projections.
4. His own attitudes to authority (that which he exercises and that which he himself obeys) need careful scrutiny.

A child is subject to the authority of his parents: they are older, bigger, stronger, more experienced and knowledgeable than he. His experience of their authority will largely colour his expectations when he goes to school, and this new experience, in turn, will modify his behaviour. Gradually, a pattern of conduct is formed and a set of attitudes becomes habitual. Some of the checks on his conduct are overthrown at adolescence, but the young person, however fiercely he asserts his independence, cannot so easily throw off the attitudinal

---

* The tensions of power are interestingly discussed in C. P. Snow's novels, especially *The Masters* and *The New Men* .

patterns which he has formed. Even his rebellion, for instance, shows his attitude. He goes forward into maturity trailing with him vestiges of earlier experience, some conscious, some unconscious, and not all necessarily consistent with one another, but liable to be reactivated in certain circumstances. The very fact that in adulthood the open checks on his conduct are fewer (his overseer or his superior officer may be no older, bigger, stronger, or wiser than he is) makes the attitudes of both the adult and his overseer of greater, not less, importance. The margin between them is less evident than in the case of children, and the adult may feel with reason that he is better than his official superior in several or most respects; it can therefore be particularly galling to feel that the other has power, even if the power is only slight, if it is not obnoxiously displayed, and if the officer as a person commands respect. (Failing these conditions, the rub is still greater.) Whether or not the situation is galling to the adult will depend largely on how sore a spot authority is to him – that is, on his attitudes.

Open or covert resentment; fear and subservience; ambivalence between resentment and subservience – these are some of the negative reactions to authority. Less obvious, perhaps, are some of the variants on acceptance of authority which may cause the powers that be less trouble, but are by no means as positive as they appear. For example, (i) undue dependence on authority; (ii) surrender of responsibility ('let him get on with it – it's his pigeon'); (iii) regarding authority as something to be placated and then circumvented (a very common attitude); (iv) 'whatever is, is right' – unwillingness to question the established order, however phoney it may be (see, for example, Whyte's criticism of acquiescence as shown in American films and fiction*): all of these are quite different from a genuine, mature acceptance.

The individual who really accepts authority is not at the mercy of childhood resentments and fears; his attitude is

* Whyte (1957, p. 234).

balanced and objective; he does not see the boss as a red rag, nor yet does he put him on a pedestal and overlook his faults – instead, he regards him as a man with a job to do and, outside that job, as not necessarily better or worse than himself. It is therefore not a personal grievance that in his work he can be told what to do, and he retains his adult independence of mind – indeed, in certain circumstances, an acceptant attitude to authority in general may be compatible with rebellion against a *particular* individual in a position of authority (the direct opposite of the unduly compliant attitudes mentioned above), and may be the final proof of the genuineness of a man's regard for authority in that he will not see it prostituted by an unworthy exemplar.

> *How happy is he born or taught*
> *Who serveth not another's will,**

is not a glorification of disobedience or of isolation, but of inner independence which may well coexist with a readiness to comply with the reasonable requirements of an outside authority, and to reject demands that are unreasonable or noxious. (It is interesting, too, that the 'servile bands' of which Wotton spoke were not imposed from outside, but came from within, and were the expression of weakness rather than of strength, that is, of ambition and will to power.) In a hierarchical situation (a large firm, a school, a hospital) a mature man will accept what Dr. G. B. Jeffery used to call 'the discipline of the situation', and will not consider himself any worse for obeying or his superior any better for being in a position to lay down requirements. In other words, he will do what he has to do without too many emotional overtones or undercurrents and without taking *personally* any slight rubs or setbacks. I say 'without too many emotional overtones or undercurrents', because a total absence of them is unlikely in practice, and indeed is hardly compatible with the unitary nature of per-

* Sir Henry Wotton.

sonality, whereby previous experiences condition what one is at present.

The difference is clear, however, between this situation and one where the emotional overtones predominate irrespective of the reality of the matter. For instance, the rebel who cannot accept authority, however reasonable, is driven by his own compulsions and is not free even when he appears to be asserting his independence, for he is enslaved to himself. There can be subjection in rebellion, as well as 'perfect freedom' in service. 'I observed that a lack of respect for authority seemed often to be founded on individual insecurity' (F.S.).

In practice, the adults one meets fall at neither extreme; and though it is unwise to rely on everyone (including oneself) being a disinterested upholder of authority, most are prepared to meet one half-way and will respond to a reasonable approach – that is, there are realistic as well as unrealistic elements to be considered. The man who is driven entirely by projections from within is as rare a bird as the one who never projects. This may seem rather a long detour to reach an obvious position, but I think the detour is worth making if it establishes the need for caution and care. With these points in mind, I shall now examine several examples.

'Attitude to authority – a tricky one this. My personal view on authority with adults is for the person in charge only to exercise it when necessary and for the rest of the time to be part of the group. . . . I have never known a friendly attitude to fail either in my time in the R.A.F. (both as an airman and as an officer) or as a Deputy Head, always provided everyone knew exactly where they stood' (F.S.). As a statement of a rational, mature person's reaction, it is unexceptionable. But I cannot help feeling that it begs a number of questions and that the tutor who took it uncritically as his guide would soon find himself a disappointed man. For it suggests, 'I have only to do this and everything will be all right', with the corollary 'If it isn't all right, it's my fault'. One can be in favour of starting off with an examination of one's own procedure and yet feel that the statement unduly weights the balance in favour of rationality. It is rather *too* straightforward, in that it neglects those irrational elements whose persistence I have described. The advice it gives is sound (a friendly attitude, be part of the group, exercise authority as little as possible, let people know where they stand), but by themselves these are not *sufficient* conditions for harmony, though they may well be necessary ones. One cannot become 'part of the group' quite so easily. The interesting sentence is the first, which as it stands is at variance with the rest, because it suggests that things are not really as simple as they seem.

It can be discouraging to a tutor to feel that everything in the garden *ought* to be lovely; and so, paradoxically, it may be an encouragement to him to have emphasis put on the likelihood of irrational projections, since this limits the responsibility which he need feel when things go wrong. (Of course, the real question is not what is encouraging or discouraging, but what most accurately represents the facts; however, the point is worth mentioning and developing.) It seems to me that a tutor would be wise to follow the advice given in the statement, but not to be unduly disappointed if the results should be less uniformly successful than the statement would suggest; and to remember that just as he can fall short of following the advice, so his students can fall short of perfect rationality in their responses. In other words, neither he nor they are *tabulae rasae*, and immoderate expectations (as suggested in a previous paragraph) are the shortest way to discouragement.*
It is better to allow some leeway for human fallibility, one's own and other people's.

An example from another field may help to clarify the point. A youth leader had worked very hard with a boy who had been in the courts, but in spite of his efforts the youth was involved in trouble again. The leader took it to heart and asked

* An excellent discussion of this point can be found in Munroe (1942, p. 339).

repeatedly 'How have I failed?' – whereas really it was not his
failure at all, but simply that the whole situation was too unfavourable. There is a sort of spiritual pride in blaming oneself
too much. It is better to compound with the facts and recognize that what one youth leader does or can do is but one element in a complex environment; and though it is his duty to do
his best, it cannot be his duty that he should succeed, since so
much is outside his control.

To relate this example to the main argument, the tutor can
reasonably do his best along the lines suggested, but he cannot
reasonably expect that he will always be successful. There is a
subtle form of nagging and overpressure (both on oneself and
on others) which comes from being conscious of one's own
virtue, and from expecting that it will always receive its due
meed of success. Beyond a certain point, it is better to let the
matter go and leave it at that.

We may now consider a second statement (notes are inserted
in square brackets). 'I think the only authority that the mature
student is willing to accept is that of someone who he knows
can help him in the pursuit of knowledge. [The keyword here
is 'mature'. Again the emphasis is on conscious rationality –
having willed the end, he is prepared to cooperate with the
means. The picture is of a steady and objective acceptance of
whatever may be necessary for him to achieve his goal.] He
belongs to the world of adults and he resents any restriction
on his freedom unless he can clearly see a reason for it. He
hates to be set tasks which appear to be irrelevant. [The check
to his rationally described purposes seems to arouse quite a
bit of irritation. In less mature persons, it may not take much
to trigger off this resentment.] He is far too polite to interrupt
[What a pity! If the work is unsuitable it might be better if he
did, as suggested in Chapter 3], walk out, or create a distur-
bance, but he will smoke or chew sweets or lounge to show his
independence. [A rather less Utopian picture now.] He likes
both constructive criticism of his work and a chance to show

that he can do better next time. [We now return to the more reasonable side, when a student is prepared to consider his studies objectively and not let self-love stand in the way of accepting help from which he can profit.] The only time I myself really felt a rebel on the course was on one occasion when I had spent a considerable time in preparing some written work on a subject I did not really understand. I handed it in with some trepidation and looked forward to its return to get some idea of where I had erred. It was returned with one small tick at the end. I was furious. In the canteen I took it out on my friend, who said, "But if she ticked it, surely it means it is all right" But I knew it wasn't' (F.S.).

The personal example with which this statement ends raises some interesting points:

1. If through mistaken delicacy (or laziness!) a tutor forbears to criticize, it may recoil on his head.

2. A student who is as objective as this one (note the honesty of 'I did not really understand' and 'I knew it wasn't') deserves better of his tutor. He is prepared to put up with some loss of self-esteem, but he is not prepared to be by-passed. What angers him here is a real grievance – the check to his rational purposes – and is not a projection of a shadowy background resentment.

3. On the other hand, it would be rash to assume that this held good of *all* students, and in other circumstances it might well be tactful and delicate, as here it was mistaken, to give just one small tick.*

4. The example raises by implication the whole topic of correction of work and, without going into this in detail, it may be well to say briefly that marking should take account of individual differences. It is a good rule that nearly everyone is working to the best of his ability and it is futile to

---

* I have been told that students discuss whether there is a correlation between size of tick and approval of contents!

depress the weaker by holding them to too high expectations (compare, too, the discussion on standards in the supervision of practical work). For this reason, I do not myself use marks or literal grades: the comparison with other students is full of pitfalls. There are better ways of letting people know how they stand, for instance, in discussion with the individual concerned. As well as differences of ability, marking should take into account questions of temperament and maturity.

5. The emphasis is not on reassurance but on facts.

Both the statements I have quoted tend (the second one less so) to gloss over the dark side of the moon, but they give a fair picture of consciously articulated attitudes to authority.

My next example is rather different in that it looks at the other side of the fence. Mr. Humber was new to the work of tutoring adults, his previous experience having been with post-graduates in a university department of education. He found working with grown-ups rather a strain, because they were 'so opinionated'. The older ones particularly 'thought they knew it all because they had been doing it some time' and 'were not ready to learn'. 'They try to tell *me*' and 'they argue' were other of his complaints. To deal with the situation, he had given the chief trouble-maker, Miss Eden, who was older than he was, a practical assignment in a particularly tough area, in the hope that this would make her more conscious of her deficiencies and so ready to accept his guidance. In conversation, Mr. Humber gave the impression of having a rather punitive attitude towards this woman, who was frustrating his efforts to bring the blessings of modern knowledge to her and who pre-ferred to remain in her own primitive state. (It may be objected that the words in this last sentence are emotively slanted and suggest an ironic way of looking at Mr. Humber, which was not in the least what *he* would have expected. I have done this deliberately, because the tale as told by him was equally slanted, in the other direction. We need to get beyond innuendo and emotive suggestion in order to consider what the realities of the situation are. I resume in a more objective tone.)

On the one side we have a middle-aged woman who has removed herself from her familiar environment, where she was successful according to her lights, and entered an unfamiliar and exacting milieu, where she may or may not make good. On any showing, that requires some courage, and the less her ability, the more courage it needs. Only a very insensitive person could fail to feel uncertain. In such a situation, some will make a bid for sympathy and support and, by proclaiming their dependence, hope to enlist the aid of authority. Others will parade their competence, it may be rather aggressively, as Miss Eden did, but feel none the less unsure. On the other side we have a tutor in his first year, keen, hardworking, enthusiastic, anxious to make a success of his new job and rather conscious that he is working by himself. He, too, has removed himself from his familiar environment where he was successful, and so on – to avoid repetition, I refer back to the beginning of the paragraph. The parallelism is complete except for a few details – the tutor can hardly make a bid for dependence, but *must* put on a parade of competence, and what may appear 'aggressive' in a student is considered merely 'a righteous display of authority' in a tutor.

Nevertheless, the parallel remains. Both, in fact, are defending tender spots, and when defensiveness is aroused, it is very difficult, as we have seen, to form an estimate of the underlying personality. Miss Eden *may* be a very difficult and truculent woman whose behaviour would be much the same however she was handled; on the other hand she may not be so – we cannot tell, since the tutor, himself uncertain and unsure (it is charitable to assume), did so much to increase her defensiveness. As in international conferences, defensiveness increases defensiveness and forms a polite euphemism for much that is downright aggression, so here on a smaller scale.

A more hopeful approach is to start at the other end and try to understand why it is that other people act as they do; and, by the same token, to be willing to examine one's own procedure and discover its determinants. These may be more similar to those of the students than one realizes. For example, when Mr. Humber said 'They try to tell *me*', the implication is that he was not willing to learn from them, yet that very unwillingness to learn was one of his charges against them. It is often useful to try to invert the situation and ask 'How would I like this myself?', and if on examination it is found that one is adopting double standards of obligation, it may be a signal that something is wrong. I do not suggest that all situations are completely reversible – there are obvious limits – but they are often more reversible than we may be prepared to admit. What is sauce for the goose is sauce for the gander, and a too-ready invocation of infallible authority for the tutor is not desirable. Criticism, like charity, begins at home. As long as Mr. Humber remains blind to his own weak spots, he is likely to be met with the sort of behaviour about which he complains.*

One of the most valuable traits that a tutor of adults can possess or seek to develop is the ability to identify imaginatively with other people, to see things through their eyes, and to attempt to consider how a situation appears to them. (It is a dangerous gift and must be kept under control, as I shall discuss in a later chapter.) Within limits, it can help enormously to try to put oneself in the other person's place, and it is far better than a display of 'authority', which so often is futile. If Mr. Humber had had more sympathetic awareness of his student's uncertainty, he might have been able to relieve it to some extent, and then it would not have been so necessary to assert his authority by placing her, like Uriah, in the thick of the battle. But when one is preoccupied with disguising one's own

*Compare Leighton (1946), particularly the sections on people and beliefs under stress.

uncertainty, there is not much margin left for recognizing that of other people.

I should like to deal briefly with margins here.* A young child can be subdued by *force majeure* but, apart from its undesirability, this becomes increasingly impracticable as he gets older. A lecturer in college or university, dealing with young students, has no leeway in size or physical strength, but he has got a margin in age, experience, and knowledge of his subject. The tutor of older students will find that this margin has shrunk considerably and, indeed, his students may have much that they can teach *him*. He is fortunate if he can recognize this fact and accept it without anxiety, and without feeling that he ought to be instructing them as a one-way process all the time. If he is able to accept it, the resulting interaction can be most valuable and may enrich both sides; but if he cannot, for whatever reason (perhaps his own conception of authority contains irrational vestiges), the lack of margin is likely to be a continuing source of insecurity. He is tempted, like Mr. Humber, to assert his authority and to rely too much on the respect due to his office. This is well enough for a time, and many a weak incumbent has been bolstered up by the position he holds (as was pointed out earlier, many people – fortunately for their superiors – are surprisingly unready to distinguish between the man and the office), but it is a poor substitute for personal respect.† In the last analysis, respect is the main foundation of the tutor's authority, and he does well to recognize that it can be secure without a constant display of fireworks on his part and without a pretension to infallibility – but the margin is a very narrow one. It may be that the margin is too narrow for him to tolerate without anxiety, and in that case he might be better suited to work with younger people. Tutor-

* Reference may also be made to Cleugh (1951), *Psychology in the Service of the School* (Chapter 5, particularly pp. 77–78).

† 'The less the personal respect received in small group relationships, the greater is the striving for the kind of impersonal respect embodied in a status judgement' (Young & Willmott, *Family and Kinship in East London*, 1957, p. 136).

ing adults is like walking near a precipice – stimulating but anxiety -provoking. An error on the tutor's part, or displays of awkward behaviour, are extra hazards that may be just too much to bear.

Here are some short examples to illustrate the points that have been made:

1. A teacher described how unhappy she had been in her first year out of college. The Head, who was a very brilliant teacher, continually came into her room with advice and criticism, and the young girl felt her confidence was sapped. As an afterthought the teacher added, 'She was a new Head.'
2. Two psychiatric social workers opened a department in a large hospital where it was a new venture. At the end of the year the one in charge was thanked by her colleague for her help, much to her surprise, since she did not feel she had given any help, but had simply left the other alone.

These two examples can be taken together. The Head, in her way, was as insecure as the young probationer; to bolster up her own security and conscious of her own excellence as a teacher, she gave more advice than the younger person could take. The psychiatric social worker left well alone and so perhaps did deserve the thanks after all. An insecure person in a position of authority is very tempted to exercise it, but it may be more conducive to the security of others if he does not do so.

3. An inexperienced tutor was very shaken by a burst of anger from a student of his own age. Surprise kept him silent, which was probably fortunate, but it was his first experience of an irrational projection and it bothered him all the more because he knew he had not much margin to meet it.
4. A more experienced tutor was cursed up hill and down dale by a very unstable student who was doing her utmost to needle her. Suddenly the student, with an indescribable mixture of malice and concern said 'I hope I haven't made

you insecure'. It was a great temptation to reply quickly – rather *too* quickly – 'No, of course not', but the student would have been well able to recognize this defensiveness for what it was. Instead, the tutor said, 'All these things you have told me need consideration. I shall have to think about them', which was probably the wisest reply in the circumstances. At any rate, it brought the rejoinder, 'It's devilish – pricking with a pin to test security', which at least suggests that the student knew perfectly well what she was doing, and that either an angry reply (to the aggression) or a defensive 'no' would have been scored by her as a victory.

In both these examples there was very little margin to spare, and it is doubtful if the tutor in (3) could have coped with the student in (4).

5. Here is an example where aggressive behaviour was directed, not against the tutor, but against another member of the group, though it is possible that the tutor might have been the target if it had appeared less risky. In this case the tutor was ten years older than the student and could hardly have seemed safe game, but the chosen victim (also older) was himself a headmaster, though of course at this time shorn of his authority. It is most unlikely that the angry young man was in the habit of behaving to his own headmaster in this way, but it does suggest that his attitudes to authority were not entirely favourable. Unfortunately the headmaster 'rose' – no doubt his own margin of tolerance was lowered at this time, just when he had no effective sanctions at his disposal – and the downtrodden masses gained a victory by proxy.

These examples are not given in order to suggest that it is *easy* for a tutor to tolerate attacks on his authority. He is only human and the natural reaction is to retaliate, particularly if he is not too sure of himself (for instance, Mr. Humber). What I

Authority

am suggesting is that the *effective* handling of a marginal situation does not lie in panic action, but rather in trying to understand what is going on, and what lies at the back of the no doubt tiresome behaviour of men and women who should have grown beyond it long ago, but apparently have not done so (and this goes for the tutor, too). As one woman pithily put it: 'After all, what is a group of adults but a group of children grown up – and some of them haven't' (F.S.). The key is to be found in the tutor's readiness to query his own actions and to put himself in the place of others.

The last topic to be taken up in this chapter concerns the more positive aspect of authority and can best be introduced in terms of Fromm's useful distinction between 'power over' and 'power to'. It may seem that I have concentrated unduly on negatives, on all the things that can go wrong, and I hope now to redress the balance. According to Fromm (1949), the leader should be regarded, not as one who has 'power over' others, with its corresponding suggestion of domination* and subjection, but as one who has 'power to' do things, that is, the emphasis is on his ability to perform certain functions. This sort of power is not a threat to others, and need evoke no defensive reaction: on the contrary, it can be used in the common service. Whatever skills the leader possesses, he uses in an outgoing manner, and his performance can be called in question just as much as that of anyone else. He is not exempt, by divine right, from criticism. What those skills are will vary from person to person, according to individual gifts (we remember the parable of the talents).

As far as tutors are concerned, the one talent that I would place highest is the ability to get the best from their students. It is, of course, very nice if a tutor is also a good lecturer, if he is of high intelligence, and if he possesses a good range of qualifications, interests, and experience.† But in the last analysis

* See also Harding (1941), *The Impulse to Dominate*.

† See, too, the discussion of the qualities desirable in a tutor of adults in the Harvard Committee report (1946), 'General Education in a Free Society', p. 261.

what counts most is not the performance of the tutor, however
excellent, but what happens to the students. The power
to generate and maintain interest in his chosen subject;
the power to encourage students so that they have confidence
in their own abilities and can work alone;* the power to stand
aside and let them go ahead on their own, not merely following
in his steps but, in favourable circumstances, surpassing in
accomplishment anything he has been able to do – these, in
ascending order of importance, are the 'powers' of a good
tutor. It is easy enough to do things along the lines of one's
abilities oneself; it is not so easy to encourage others to pro-
ductive activity, yet in this lies the justification of the tutor.

The statements quoted earlier in this chapter had the germ
of the distinction in them: authority in the sense of 'power
over' is a side issue and is to be used sparingly; authority in the
sense of function or 'power to' is stressed in the second statement as being the only acceptable kind. The function of the
tutor is to help his students to realize their potentialities; it is
not to stand on his own dignity and allow it to get in the way
of more important concerns – his dignity will be all the safer if
he is not preoccupied with it.†

So we come back full circle to the simplicity of 'we are all
people'; if he remembers this, the tutor will be more tolerant
of the weaknesses that irritate him in his students, knowing
that he shares them too. Otherwise, if he misinterprets the
meaning of 'authority', he is only too likely to end with the
despairing cry of Danton on his way to execution: 'It were better
to be a poor fisherman than to meddle in the governing of men.'‡

* 'The most permanently helpful influence is that which stimulates others to activity
on their own part and leads them to form their own opinions, think their own
thoughts, and live their own lives' (Badley, *Memories & Reflections*, 1955, p. 109).

† 'Poise comes from an inner reserve, from a clarity and conviction as to purpose.
Without these, personal force is apt to degenerate into that flashy and indeterminate
thing miscalled "personality"' (Harvard Committee report, 1946, p. 173).

‡ Quoted by Leighton (1946) in *The Governing of Men*.

Chapter Eight

POINTS OF VIEW

GENERAL statements must be constantly tested out by reference to examples, and for that reason it seemed desirable to give at this stage an account of the working-out of one particular tutorial situation. It is easy enough to enunciate well-meaning advice to others, but it is what happens in the actual interplay between student and tutor that provides the real test.

Mrs. Severn was a student of thirty-five. She had a very good social manner, an attractive appearance, and considerable ability. She had done well in other work before taking emergency training as a teacher, and since then all reports on her spoke favourably of her energy and drive, the high standards she set herself, and the excellent results she gained from the children. With these strong recommendations, it was a considerable surprise to her tutor how tense and hostile she seemed at her first tutorial. There was nothing in the content of the interview to cause this and the tutor ruefully regarded it as a warning of squalls ahead. They soon came.

October 19. In her second tutorial she gave a long story of her life, at top speed, and in a hard, detached tone which showed the effort she was making to maintain control. (It is unusual for family backgrounds and details of personal history to be divulged at such a very early stage, and the effect was as if she was serving notice that she could be difficult.) She was one of two children; her father had been an invalid and unable to work for some years — he had died when she was eleven. In the upheaval before and after this she had been sent about among relatives, never really wanted, and her education had suffered. Her sister, much older, had been less affected by the unsettlement and had done well at school. There was considerable poverty and she left school as soon as she could. Her mother (from the sound of it as dogged and determined as she was herself) had done wonders to keep things going, for there were also two old grandparents. She married in the war, but her husband was killed almost immediately. Later extracts from the tutor's records* follow (notes are inserted):

November 5. Says has faced her problems. Critical tone when speaking of her mother. Further details re family.

November 13. Essay back – edgy and anxious. Burst of relief when told it was good.

November 18. Seen in practical work at school. Aggressive – bickering with other students.

November 28. Pressed hard for direct suggestions – seemed very angry when tutor avoided giving any.[1]

[1] The tutor felt that her attitude to authority was so ambivalent that to accede would only have stored up more resentment (see Chapter 5).

December 19. Brought her work (unasked for) and inquired very aggressively if it was right . . .

TUTOR How are things going? (*Aggression vanished.*)

MRS. S I'm very tired, but that's not unusual. I always spend the first days of the holiday in tears.

TUTOR Could you take it more easily?[2]

MRS. S I always go hard at everything. It would mean crossing myself out and starting again.

[2] The first appearance of a theme that was to recur constantly.

* The records were written up from memory, usually at the end of the same day. No attempt was made at a verbatim account, but key sentences were usually reproduced and the gist of the intervening conversation summarized. It is believed that the record is a reasonably accurate statement of the development of the situation as seen by the tutor.

January 8. Anxiety in taking intelligence test (N.B. good ability, little formal education).

January 15. Edgy and ambivalent. Asked for tutorial – straightforward on whole. Said she came on course as ammunition against her headmaster.[3]

[3] Anti-authority.

January 17. Direct attack on tutor in lecture.[4] Wanted to know definitely what to do.

[4] A very rare occurrence.

January 24. (*After a bad lecture, tutor chastened.*) MRS. S It gives us a chance of seeing how a lecturer accepts failure.[5]

[5] Students will naturally observe this with interest. Tutors commonly expect students to accept deflation gracefully: but what sort of example do we ourselves set?

January 29.

> TUTOR Are you keeping your head above water?
> MRS. S Yes, much better this term.
> TUTOR Good. Take it easy.
> MRS. S It's only *just* above water, but it is above. (*Seems steadier and more relaxed, in spite of brick on 17th.*)

January 30. Seen in school. Took criticism pleasantly. Tutor emboldened to ask cautiously whether she was inclined to drive the children.

> MRS. S No, I'm not a driver. . . . (*later*) It would be foolish to go my own way because I came here for expert advice.
> TUTOR Wouldn't it be better if you followed your own judgement instead of depending so much on what others tell you?[6]
> MRS. S No, I can do that any time. I haven't got much confidence[7] – anyway, it's silly to be oversure.
> TUTOR Confidence isn't being cocksure.

[6] A note made at the time adds – 'I wasn't at all sure of the wisdom of starting this issue. It may have been a subtle overpressure to expect independence from this student, and anyway her position was reasonable.'

[7] An important remark. Probably very true. Gives *impression* of bustling confidence.

January 31. Suddenly very desirous of changing plan of work – wanted permission[8] (*much emphasized*). Tutor temporized, asked why she thought this a good idea, finally gave opinion that it was unnecessary but she could do it if she wished. Edgy.

Later same day.

> TUTOR On the point you raised, I think it's unwise but I shall be delighted if you do it, because you would be following your own judgement and not mine.
>
> MRS. S I was thinking I'd do it in spite of all and never mind if you don't like it.[9]
>
> TUTOR You put such stress on permission granted and withheld – then it's my fault if it's wrong.
>
> MRS. S No, but I had a very dominating mother and this is the result – I can't get clear of it.[10] . . . I know I have to be careful or I'd dominate the children.[11] Even if this choice is not the wisest, I think it's best for my own development.[12]
>
> TUTOR Yes . . . work good, no need to be worried.
>
> MRS. S But it's quite irrational, I know that.[13] My mother always praised my sister's ability – I lost confidence, but later realized I'm as intelligent as she was. . . . (*Continued with long story about family.*)
>
> TUTOR As far as these things are rational, which they aren't, you've good ability and should be all right if you go on more easily, as I think you've been doing this term.
>
> MRS. S Yes, much better this term.

[8] No permission was needed.   [9] A very considerable step forward.
[10] A very sudden outburst. It suggests that she is well aware of her difficulties in an authority situation. Throws interesting light on the persistence into adult life of childhood attitudes, as discussed in the previous chapter.
[11] Contradicts remark of previous day. She is now able to admit her own tendencies to dominate.

[12] Consolidating note 9 and giving reason for it – good insight. Again contradicts remark of previous day – apparently overpressure discussed in note 6 hasn't done any harm; it must have come when she was ready to move forward anyway.
[13] Again good insight.

[It is interesting to note the clustering of entries in the record. At this point they are very frequent, almost as if she were working up to a climax, and then they drop away sharply. The entries for the rest of the term are few and brief. It may also be added here that she made her change and it turned out very successful.]

March 3. My crazy upbringing. . . . (At own school) I fight but I don't always win.[14]
[14] A less truculent reference than note 3?

March 7. Late and tense at meeting to discuss plans for block teaching. Visiting lecturer picked her out in group as being very aggressive (another visitor last week had picked her out as able).

Summer term
April 24. Overcritical of school where she is doing block teaching, but peaceful in herself.
April 26. Refused to go off sick – 'fear it would be thought a flight into illness' (the last person of whom this would be suspected).
April 29. Seen in school. Ought to have been away – bullied doctor into letting her stay. Ditto with tutor – it seemed lesser of two evils.

MRS. S I daren't be away and lose revision time. It would be a worse strain to stay away because I'd worry. I've put everything I've got into taking this course. I can't rub my whole personality out and take things gently.[15] More strain during emergency training than now – just the same attitudes came up then and it's interesting to me to realize this.[16] I think I can go through now without undue strain

or flop at the end. I don't find teaching a strain[17] –
I enjoy it. I know I've been overworking. . . .
Tutor suggested that she might take things more easily with
the children.

    MRS. S It wouldn't work at all, would be chaos (*returned to this later and seemed more ready to consider it*). I couldn't stand really badly behaved children. Strict discipline of mother (*referred to twice*).

Amiably accepted criticisms.

[15] Compare remark of December 19.
[16] Reactivation of attitudes during earlier training is common.
[17] But see comment of December 19 re tears.

May 15.

    MRS. S School is a bit better but I find it very difficult to accept the low standards of the children. Am I wrong in thinking they could do better? It's a slack school.

    TUTOR Probably six of you and half a dozen of them. You may be right about the school, but could you ease off on the children?

    MRS. S I think I have done,[18] but it seems awful to me.

(*Topic of children's behaviour continued for some time, until tutor brought it back.*)

    TUTOR When I came to see you in school I felt helpless, because I could see what most needed to be done, but had no idea how to achieve it – for you to ease off yourself. It's easy for someone to say 'take it easy', but it must be very irritating when temperamentally you take it hard.[19]

    MRS. S If I took it easy I wouldn't be here – going all out – at limit of my powers (*continued to argue that*

> *she had no alternative – rather apologetic for arguing,*
> *not hostile).*

Tutor took factual line – diminishing returns when over-tired.[20]

MRS. S   I'm under pressure – daren't slacken – *you* wouldn't either.

TUTOR   I would. I'd say: 'Be blowed – I'm off.'

MRS. S   I've a slow mind and a poor memory. I *can't* do otherwise.[21]

[18] Evidently she *had* been ready to consider the suggestion.

[19] An attempt was made here to see things from Mrs. Severn's point of view, not just to give advice, however justified.

[20] There was real chance of this.

[21] This remark is true, but not for the reason she gave. However, as long as she believed her reason, it would prevent any easing off. At this point, the tutor remembers clearly a feeling of utter hopelessness – a long vista of previous attempts on this theme rose up, each with its slightly encouraging comment 'seems more relaxed'. 'much better this term'; and yet, in sum, although this was May, there was no advance on December. It was like a gramophone record that had stuck and repeated the same message endlessly. Time was short, and as they rose to go, one last attempt was made.

Tutor gave example of running desperately for a train which *must* be caught.

MRS. S   But that's my point exactly. You're arguing on my side.

TUTOR   But you have time to spare.[22]

MRS. S   (*Pause, slowly*) You have more confidence in my abilities than I have.[23]

TUTOR   If I had felt you couldn't do it, in the circumstances, knowing you were strained, I would have told you. Would it help if you had sufficient confidence that I would tell you if you couldn't?

MRS. S   (*Complete change of tone*) Yes, very much – that would do it.[24]

TUTOR   And if you are easier you will find the children also easier.[25]

In the group meeting that followed this, Mrs. S looked excited, thoughtful, relieved.

[22] This simple remark at last went home.

[23] The crucial realization that the tutor *genuinely* felt she could relax *safely* (contrast the number of times she had previously been told that her work was good).

[24] Decisive solution. Tutor wondered afterwards as to wisdom of giving blank cheque in this way, but thought on the whole that the circumstances justified it, particularly since Mrs. Severn seemed *sure* it would help.

[25] A parting shot!

June 13.

MRS. S I don't need to be told how to revise – I've decided to do a bit and then call it a day. If I go down the drain, then I do, but it's no good trying to do more than I can – must make best of myself and keep my head clear. . . .[26] School went better and I had an easy relationship with the children – quite sorry to leave – got work from them at their level, not at level I thought they should do.[27] You were quite right in saying it was partly me as well as them. When I go back to my own job I shall have a gentle fight[28] with my headmaster to bring his expectations to a suitable level.

[26] It all sounds simple now, but the gap between *saying* something and *realizing* it appears to have been crossed. She is now accepting what in note 15 and note 21 she said she couldn't.

[27] One test of an easier attitude is that it spreads into other situations (see note 25).

[28] Compare notes 3 and 14.

June 14. Rather aggressive in group.

June 15. Hung on to own point of view in group discussion – open contradiction of tutor[29] (a matter of opinion, not of fact).

[29] This wasn't aggressive. It represents a further consolidation of the development noted in notes 9 and 12.

June 19. I've stopped being bad.

June 20. I shall stop revising three days before the examination.

June 27. I didn't like the first exam. I wonder if it's any good going on? (*Wasn't seriously thinking of withdrawing.*)

So far, the account has been given entirely from the point of view of the tutor. But that is by no means the whole of the story, for Mrs. Severn saw it quite differently. She read the tutor's account above and agreed to add her side of the matter. By her generous cooperation, the value of the material has been immeasurably increased since it helps us to see something of a second dimension. The account that follows has been pieced together from her verbal and written comments – she says that as far as she knows she has been absolutely honest in them. A general statement of her feelings at the beginning of the course is followed by her (lettered) notes on particular points.

When she came, she says, she had no real idea of her own ability, for it had never been put to the test of a formal examination and, although she had done well on her emergency course, there was always the fear that perhaps a lower standard was permitted just because of the emergency: university work would be quite another matter. At the same time, there was a strong drive to succeed, and to exercise powers that she felt she possessed; subconsciously, too, there may have been an urge to prove to herself that the frustrations of her childhood need not debar her permanently from learning.

To this intellectual ambivalence, further disturbing cross-currents were added by the cumulative emotional effect of her unsettled and yet strict upbringing. Herself naturally forceful and outgoing, she had been very much kept at heel, even when she was adult, with outward compliance masking an inward mixture of uncertainty and striving towards self-determination.

With all these conflicting feelings, she arrived at the course expectant, anxious, and keyed up. She was extremely nervous at her first tutorial, though she did her best to cover it with a show of confidence. 'I came out feeling very inadequate and as though I'd been talking to a completely detached and impersonal tutor. Rather as though I was a worm on a pin which did not come up to expectation. A very unusual experience for me, I usually am able to make contact with people very quickly.' She found the tutor unwilling to answer her requests for clarification, and this impression of unhelpfulness persisted for some weeks. With an unclear impulse that if she told the tutor more about herself it would justify her position, she launched on her account of her childhood, struggling as she did so against 'a mixture of nervousness and disturbed feeling arising from being hit on my most vulnerable spot – feeling of inadequacy'.

A An early experience in the group, where the tutor jumped heavily on another student, increased her fearfulness, for how dreadful it would be if this happened to her!
[The tutor has completely forgotten the incident and could not recall it even when details were given. It is a good example of how errors, of which one is unaware, can be held against one, and bedevil relationships for some time.]
B In her turn, Mrs. Severn did not recollect the incidents (all allegedly aggressive) of November 18, November 28, and January 17.
[The notorious unreliability of memory and its tendency to overlook inconvenient episodes are illustrated here – by both sides. The final example (January 17) is particularly interesting. It is quite clear that no attack was intended. Yet because Mrs. Severn landed heavily on what was in fact a weak point, the tutor *felt* it as an attack. This is exactly the same mechanism as that which caused Mrs. Severn to write 'being *hit* on my most vulnerable spot'. One's own vulnerability makes one touchy. Tutors need to remember that they can unjustly attribute fancied offences to students, and that similarly they will be unjustly blamed themselves.]
C (See note 3 above). Mrs. Severn felt that the interpretation of January 15 was completely unfair, in that it depended on

a single remark taken out of context. She said, 'I'm *sure* you're barking up the wrong tree at this point – it's a glaring instance of selection gone wrong'.

Mrs. Severn made several comments on the entry for January 31:

D (note 8). Others beside herself thought permission was required.

E (note 10). 'I *am* aware that because in childhood my mother dominated us almost out of existence, I have to be careful not to be a yes-man and then resent it inwardly.' [Compare with this the tutor's early hunch – note 1.]

F (note 11). She makes a distinction between dominating and driving – hence no contradiction.

Mrs. Severn's next comments concern the entry for April 29:

G (note 16). 'In both my attempts to acquire training, emotionally I revert to a childish level and find myself inwardly fighting the early feeling of inadequacy and rejection. . . . I think this is an *extremely* important point. This reversion is devastating to an adult. One seems to lose so much of the ground gained in development that just the loss itself brings insecurity in addition to the return of childish insecurity.'

H (note 17). She makes a distinction between fatigue and strain. She wouldn't consider being overtired an indication of strain.

The important interview of May 15 brings two comments:

I (note 19). 'I felt you really *were* sympathetic and understood my difficulty.'

J (note 22). 'I respected your judgement. I felt that you were really saying, "You have enough ability to get through", which led me to make my next remark. It was more asking *have* you this confidence in my ability. Your reply was most reassuring for in myself I felt inadequate.'

к (note 28). Previously she had been unsure of her ground, but now (June 13) she felt ready to tackle her headmaster. [The opposite interpretation of 'gentle fight' to that given by the tutor.]

Points of view could, of course, be multiplied indefinitely – for instance, in the group Mrs. Severn appeared lively, popular, rather bossy – and it is not suggested that the two aspects here set out give the whole picture between them; but the confrontation of the two accounts is extremely illuminating and raises issues of some importance, which I shall now discuss.

(i). Since memory is so deceptive, there is much to be said in favour of making written notes, if there is any likelihood of a need of accurate recall later (for instance, it is sometimes important to be sure of the exact sequence of events, and a dated record is the only way of avoiding doubt). Naturally, no tutor would wish or be able to keep notes as full as those above on *every* member of his class; my own practice is to make full notes only where they are required administratively, or for purposes of a study on which I am engaged, or to help me when it is necessary to try to walk delicately. Proper selection can prevent records from being burdensome, but their practical and theoretical value is unquestionable.

In this example, the advantages of having a continuous record over a period of time are that quite small details can appear significant when seen in context, and that small changes which otherwise would be missed can be observed. (No assumption as to the *causes* of the changes is involved: the record simply notes the present position on each occasion, like temperature readings.) At the same time, the record shows clearly that progress is uncertain and uneven – there are dramatic episodes of change, backslidings, long uneventful weeks, reactivation of earlier situations, consolidation – but at least in the finish Mrs. Severn completed the course successfully and did not 'flop' afterwards.

(ii). But tutors' records are not infallible. They give one side only of the story, and the student's point of view is left as the dark side of the moon, never visible.

Furthermore, there is a tendency towards selective perception (see notes C and K above) which can give a misleadingly smooth 'finish' to the tutor's picture, a tidying out of sight of inconvenient loose ends. Also, it is easy to slide over from facts to interpretations and explanations and, in doing so, to introduce still more tidying. If this is true even in a relatively careful record, it is still more true of the haphazard unthinking way in which people normally arrive at their opinions.* I think this point should be stressed to the utmost; and it does us, as tutors, no harm to reflect occasionally on the precariousness of the judgements which we necessarily make in the course of doing our work.

(iii). But there is more than logic involved, and I do not mean to suggest that the precariousness of judgements should be the last word. Communication between people is extremely subtle and delicate, with a considerable intuitive and empathic element. Mrs. Severn's feelings at her first tutorial have now been described; what came over to the tutor was something like this – '?', 'What have we here?' 'More in this than meets the eye'. Corroboration came very swiftly, in the information given at the next tutorial. Mrs. Severn now suggests that, just as the unrest of her feelings (under a very assured social manner) was 'caught' by the tutor, so in turn she picked up the tutor's '?' and unconsciously responded to it by providing some answers on the next occasion. This extremely perceptive suggestion is of great interest in showing the speed and subtlety of communication, even in the absence of contact. It could explain why Mrs. Severn said so much, although sympathy was felt to be lacking.

* For further discussion of this point, see Cleugh (1951), *Psychology in the Service of the School*, Chapter 2, or any book on logic.

Obviously it is not susceptible of 'proof', but it seems to be very plausible.

(iv). In view of the evidence given here, the present fashion for interpreting to others the 'meaning' of their actions needs to be seriously called in question. How many accounts in books and journals do we not read where it is blithely taken for granted that the writer's interpretation is absolutely and completely correct? What is the justification for such an assumption? Pseudo-analytical activity by unqualified persons – quite apart from the question of damage – can so easily be mistaken. The fact that an interpretation hangs together and is internally coherent may merely mean, not that it *must* be correct, but that selective smoothing has occurred.

(v). A more immediately practical reflection that this material may induce in tutors is the unwisdom of taking behaviour at its face value. The record shows the gradual realization by the tutor that, as well as the immediately apparent aggressiveness, there was a problem of confidence. Mrs. Severn adds: 'A façade of confidence, giving an impression of aggression, frequently has been built up to cover extreme diffidence and nervousness. . . . There may be a danger in mistaking the façade for aggression. Is it not true that some tutors unwisely would have tackled me outright as aggressive? At which I would have put my tail between my legs and run.' It is worth while remembering that (a) the behaviour complained of may be defensive in origin (as in this case); (b) there is room for more than one opinion as to what that behaviour is (for example, Mrs. Severn did not realize that she appeared aggressive, though she agreed that other people in previous situations had sometimes considered her so); (c) the tutor's point of view is not necessarily right.

(vi). There is need for considerable tolerance of manifestations of insecurity caused by strange surroundings and removal from ordinary routine. Mrs. Severn makes this point very strongly (note G) and it is one which has been made to me by several other former students (see also the example of Mr. Humber and Miss Eden in the previous chapter). Insecurity must be considered a normal reaction which every tutor can expect to meet, though naturally its severity will depend on circumstances. Overseas students, for example, have a more total readjustment to make than those who are living at home, and students on a full-time course than those on a part-time one.

(vii). Detailed studies of individuals are as a rule only available when those individuals are in some way unusual. But a great deal can be learned by a similarly careful study of normal personalities (as is done, for instance, by R. W. White (1953) in *Lives in Progress* or, at the group level, by the Tavistock researches into normal families). Not all students are as articulate or as frank as Mrs. Severn but, apart from that, many parallels to her can be found in classes of adults; for that reason, it seemed well worth while to consider in detail the mechanisms of that interaction between person and person which is at the root of all real teaching.

Chapter Nine

CHANGE OF ATTITUDES

WHEN I WAS considering the topic of this chapter, I asked some of my former students for their comments. One man stated roundly: 'The effect of an educational experience in adult life is to modify one's attitude in some way. If there is no modification there has been only a wasted experience.' In view of the common belief that plasticity decreases as people become older, that might appear a rather depressing prospect for adult education. For how far in fact is change genuine? It is, as another respondent put it, 'possible that people whose attitudes appear greatly modified are for the first time for a number of years in a position where they can give experience to beliefs and practices which they have always thought to be right but which circumstances – or inertia – have prevented them from using.'

As against this merely apparent change, a third comment says that a genuine change in people involves 'a different attitude to the *same circumstances* as framed their previously held attitudes. They are different – the world remains the same. Broadly speaking, they can be split into two classes: (i) those with a sufficient mastery of techniques to put into operation the full weight of their new outlook (it would be interesting to know if there are many); (ii) those who lack sufficient technique or confidence to carry through the full operation of their new ideas (circumstances may be adverse too). Class (i) have chosen a new road, they walk along it; eventually it becomes as familiar as the old – it may become a different rut – but they have been permanently affected. Class (ii) can be split into two groups: (a) those who know what they would like to do but are overweighed by their own inadequacy or circumstances, and eventually sink back into the old ways. The change has been real, but becomes superficial in practice; (b) those who, while not completely master of themselves and circumstances, endeavour to change their methods as far as they are able, constantly acquire new strengths and practise them, and hold fast to their ideals.' I have quoted this at length because, though framed in terms of different methods of teaching, it raises issues of more general application (at least as old as the parable of the sower) in the limitations placed on change by competence and by outside circumstances.

A fourth respondent said: 'Sometimes we resist modification of attitudes through past training or tradition and through natural conservatism. Modification can be going on but we maintain the same forms. Then intellectual justification for change may be seen. There is now no objection to modification, but it still doesn't happen quickly, but comes slowly. Causes – real experience, possibility of free choice. It can't be hurried, neither can it be other than from within. . . . If there were a sudden change, I would expect it to be temporary. Most change is in the same direction and is more or less development, but I would not discount the possibility of a great change over a long period under favourable conditions.'

Finally, a woman whom I shall call Miss Dee, wrote: 'I regard the problems of encouraging the persistence of newly acquired attitudes as being of a more obviously practical nature, such as favourable environmental circumstances and so on', and she therefore preferred to consider the *inner* factors which might prevent or facilitate a change of attitude. Among unfavourable factors she included: (i) a rigid personality structure; (ii) resistance at a low level of accessibility, too low for contemporary reasons and emotions to have any effect; (iii) precarious personality equilibrium – any change is seen as a threat to security. 'The awkward students in lectures were usually those who felt the new thinking demanded of them to be an attack on sensitive parts.' She considered the favourable factors to be: (i) 'a self-concept wrapped round adjustability', that is, involving flexibility as an ideal; (ii) group approval and support – very necessary at a time of considerable psychological discomfort; (iii) time – any lasting change needs consolidating; (iv) the experience of tremendous relief which accompanies the surrendering of an old attitude for a new one more in accordance with reason and new knowledge; (v) a sensible attitude to the success-failure pattern; a change of attitude necessarily involves an admission of error and of long-standing error, too; (vi) deliberate and self-critical awareness (might only apply to certain types of people); (vii) an emotional impact – most commonly observed in temporary conversions, but can be permanent. Miss Dee gave as an example her own attitude to the deaf, which changed as a result of a sudden empathic realization of their social isolation, after a visit to a school for deaf children. Miss Dee concluded: 'We do change our attitudes however slightly, continuously, whether we like it or not. Old people, who have come to realize how these long slow changes have affected them, are often less prejudiced and more psychologically elastic than middle-aged people, who I suppose are struggling with more resistance within themselves.'

I propose, in this chapter, to exemplify some points that these men and women have raised, first with reference to the material set out in the last chapter and then with other illustrations.

Returning to the story of Mrs. Severn, I shall examine how far genuine changes took place, in relation to the three main issues that came up – attitudes to authority, confidence, tension.

First of all, it must be stressed that a false appearance of change can be given which is simply a result of getting to know people better. A defensive and suspicious attitude (for example, in face of authority) may melt away after a time without any real change: it is a reaction to a new situation and as the situation becomes familiar the defensiveness is no longer needed – but in the next new situation it will quickly reappear. Teachers at all levels have a continual temptation to overestimate how much 'better' their charges have become in their care, for this reason, but the underlying attitude persists unaltered. On the other hand, the apparent change may be for the worse – as, for instance, when Mrs. Severn's façade of confidence was replaced by uncertainty and anxiety. It would be just as unreasonable to blame the tutor for this as it is to give him credit for the pseudo-improvement involved in settling down: in neither case has there been an alteration in attitude. I would therefore regard with caution any claims that a genuine change had taken place which were based *only* on the improvement in Mrs. Severn's attitude to the authority of the tutor, though there certainly seemed to be such an improvement.

It is to be remembered that adults have had many years of learning responses which finally become their habitual attitudes, and it is not to be expected that such responses will be easily modified or unlearned. Certainly it would be unwise to claim too much in this respect, and the surprising thing is that *any* modification takes place. But I believe that it does, not at the deepest levels that are the province of the psychiatrist and that are not in question here, and not, on the other hand, in purely superficial terms. The intermediate level of change that is involved here can best be considered as the impact of a genuine experience upon a person.

Take, for instance, the gap between the constant iteration to Mrs. Severn that her work was good and her inability to realize this at an operational level (alternatively, one can say that she *knew* it to be good, but could not *feel* that it was). It was the closing of the gap by a genuine realization that was the important thing, and here we can speak only in metaphors – it 'went home', 'something clicked', 'she fused',* 'it got across', 'insight'. All these metaphors have in common the idea of a real experience, integrating previously diverse elements, and perhaps this is as far as we can go in the language of prose, though mystics and poets might take it further. It is this experience which is at the base of real teaching, the ability to communicate without loss of value, because, as we all know to our cost, nearly always something is lost in the process of communication. If it were not so, if output and intake corresponded, how easy teaching would be! It might almost be said that the art of teaching is to communicate across a gap; and here I include self-teaching, which is what was involved in Mrs. Severn's case. One way of putting it would be to say that she was re-educating herself, and that a genuine alteration in attitudes involves a regrouping of experience, a fresh perception of the self in its relation to the external world. Essentially, it is a process which the individual must do for himself, and it is how *he* regards the world which is the key – not how he ought to regard it, or what the situation in fact is, but how it appears to him. This is well brought out in the example of Mrs. Severn: as long as she felt 'I can't do otherwise' (see note 21), then she could not, and it would be beside the point for another person to think that *the facts alone* of her ability could disprove her. One so easily tends to assume that an able student must be aware of his competence, whereas in my experience I have frequently noted that such a one is self-critical and perhaps diffident. Of course, 'the facts' have their use and value, and I do not want to appear to be upholding an extreme phenomenalist position, but the crux here is how they can be brought into relation with Mrs. Severn's perception of herself. Once this had

* This metaphor was suggested by Forster in *The Longest Journey* (1907, p. 202), where the superficiality of Agnes is underlined by a comparison with the electric light. 'Click, she's on. Click, she's off. No waste, no flicker. I wish she'd fuse.' Presumably, fusing is the only chance of a real conflagration. This metaphor, in my thinking, has become mixed with the other meaning, of fusion of metals. So do words set traps for thoughts and, at the same time, suggest new ideas through metaphor.

occurred, she did actually do what she said she was unable to do (note 26). It seems unquestionable that this was a genuine change and not a mere artifact of the kind discussed earlier.

Mrs. Severn comments: 'I think my emergency training began the change of attitude. That and my university experience finally helped me to a fresh perception of myself in relation to the external world. I had through all my post-adolescent life seen myself through my mother's and sister's eyes. . . . I feel I have gained confidence to persuade gently and patiently those who are working with me, and so I hope the children will benefit.'

The suggestion is that change can come about as a sort of self-education: what, then, is the part played by others in this process? There is a stimulating article by Staines (1958), in which he shows how young children gradually build up a picture of the sort of people they are from the behaviour, comments, and references to them of others around, and the work of Jersild (1955) is also relevant here. But by far the most systematic studies of this whole territory are those of Rogers and his associates,* and their explanation of personality changes among normal adults is of vital importance. Other people can help or hinder, but the essential reorientation is from within: thus, in the example given, the process was started by the simple remark 'you have time to spare', and the tutor's part could be thought of as that of a catalyst, facilitating the emergence of the realization that this was indeed so – but until Mrs. Severn realized it *herself*, no progress was made.† When she *did* realize it herself she was able to let go and ease off on her self-defeating efforts; this suggests that, basically, she had found some confidence from somewhere, for without confidence it would not

* See Rogers (1942, 1948, 1951); Rogers & Dymond (1954); Snyder (1947); and Snygg & Combs (1949).

† Mrs. Severn herself added an excellent illustration of this. When her sister heard of her university success, she said: 'And *this* was the girl who couldn't pass the 11+'. Mrs. Severn suddenly realized that her feeling of intellectual incompetence stemmed back to this *and was baseless*. Here the sister is the catalyst, but the realization still has to be Mrs. Severn's own.

have been possible. The two issues, of confidence and release of tension, are thus interconnected here.

A further point to notice in passing is that confidence can be on several levels: on the surface, Mrs. Severn would pass as a bright confident person, below this was considerable uncertainty and anxiety, but in the last analysis her confidence held.* It is noteworthy also that when she was able to bring herself to depend on her own judgement (notes 9 and 12) success followed, and this would help in building up confidence for the future.

The first step, on which later progress depended, was the freeing of herself from the shackles of the too-dominating authority which she had internalized (as distinct from the actual control of her actions by her mother, which had long since been given up). Whatever her mother was like in reality, there seems no doubt that Mrs. Severn's *concept* of authority was of domination – hence the alternate over-compliance and resentment which caused difficulties in her relations with authority figures. No one but herself could bring about the revision† of that concept, but the process could be helped or hindered by the actions of those figures. It was thus important for the tutor to avoid confirming the stereotype of controlling force (note E). Non-intervention from the tutor was naturally resented as lack of support, but it forced Mrs. Severn back on her own resources, which were in fact perfectly adequate though she did not *feel* that they were. From the point of view of tutors, the moral seems to be that one should not be *too* ready to take over the responsibility for choice which is properly the students' as long as they are able to make the choice themselves – which brings us back full circle to the point in Chapter 5 where it was first made.

Finally, Mrs. Severn said some years later that her greatly increased confidence enabled her to *exercise* authority and meet

* Not to mention the marked degree of basic confidence entailed in her allowing this material to go forward for publication.

† Literally, re-vision.

criticism more tolerantly and patiently – which suggests that alteration in her concept of authority had also occurred.

Change, however, takes place only within limits, within the context, so to speak, of one's potentialities (for example, Mrs. Severn does not cease to be forceful and downright). The notion of *range* is helpful here. It is possible to widen one's experience and tolerance of the strange and the unexpected, and in so doing find that one possessed talents of which one was unaware, but there must be a limit to this process. Conversely, within the range of what *is* possible, there are some things which one does better than others, and it seems only common sense to try to concentrate on those of optimum facility and success. An example will explain what I mean.

Miss Trent, who had taught normal children for some years, took a post with an unstable problem class: as anyone would, she found it heavy going. It was reasonable that she should wish to extend her experience and, until she had tried it, how could she know whether it was her line or not? Unfortunately, having attempted it, she felt herself in honour bound to succeed – anything else would be 'giving in', and she felt she should never do that; so she struggled on for some time in work that was uncongenial. The same rigid and moralistic approach which she adopted towards herself she also attempted to adopt towards the children, without realizing that this in itself made her particularly unsuitable to deal with such children. She was, in fact, trying to go outside her range, instead of being content with something else which she could have done better.

On the other hand, a successful attempt to widen one's range can bring benefits in increased confidence and skill. In the following detailed example, a man made a very gallant attempt to widen his range, and it may be all the more instructive for not being uncloudedly a success story. It can serve to test the hypothesis of the part of the tutor being that of a catalyst, and it also ties in with some of the remarks made earlier regarding the supervision of practical work. The material, as before, is taken from the tutor's record (and annotated) and is used with the permission of the subject, for which I am extremely grateful.

May 2. Things were not going too well when the supervisor visited Mr. Mersey, a man in his mid-forties, working with a class of 8-year-olds. He was a clever man who found it difficult to get the children's level and he felt that if he gave an inch they would take an ell. The tutor said that in fact they *hadn't* taken advantage when they were fully occupied and when he worked with them and not against them: that it wasn't necessary always to rule with an iron hand. The tutor ended by saying 'I'm not advocating a free-for-all.'

M. I know you wouldn't do that.

Said he agreed with general reading of the situation.[1]

[1] He doesn't seem to have been antagonized so far.

May 4.

M. I want some specific help. My diagnosis is that I'm afraid of losing discipline. . . .

(Tutor asked whether it would be worth trying working with the children instead of clamping down on them.)

M. Will make a genuine effort to try permissiveness – if I don't then I can't.

T. Range can be extended but not indefinitely.

M. My range is rather narrow. I'm too earnest.

T. It seems unfair that other people can achieve things with so little effort when you try so hard. Need for light touch. . . .

M. Not easy to teach when others present, though I didn't feel you were hostile.

T. I didn't think I put you off.

M. No. What you saw was a fair cross-section, neither better nor worse than usual.[2]

[2] These exchanges appear to have established that both are working together on a common problem. There doesn't seem to be any resentment of the tutor, apart from the very natural unwillingness to be seen at a disadvantage. There is no attempt to gloss over difficulties, on either side.

He *asks* for help – no defensiveness. Good contact. Tutor gives a definite lead – advisable in this case (contrast Mrs. Severn). Note that last remark establishes level of work – important for tutor to know this.

May 9.

    M. I've eased off – had to for my own sake – was getting very worried. Not sleeping. But the children don't meet you half-way – why should only I modify?

    T. Doesn't seem fair? They aren't keeping bargain?[3]

    M. But they didn't make a bargain.[4]

    T. Result may not come for some years.

    M. One doesn't like to think one is so rigid that it takes two years to change.

    T. But you're an adult – it would be superficial if you *did* alter easily.[5]

    M. One has believed in child-centred education for years. . . .[6] Headmaster standing over children is effective in the short run but not really.

(Later reported to have said: Some of us would *like* to be directed.)

[3] Tutor responds to the implied complaint.
[4] He is objective enough to see that he hasn't really a complaint.
[5] No good pretending it is going to be easy.
[6] But not at the operative level – a good example of the gap between saying and meaning. Next remark more indicative of genuine realization.

May 30. Seen again in school. Rather patchy – children bubbly, unsuitable material and methods, gaps in organization.

    M. I want to do the right thing, what I'm expected to do. Anxious when I first started teaching twenty years ago – we had no help with method – felt unsure. Help me and tell me what to do.[7] Am a thoroughly old-fashioned teacher.

(Note: It should be stressed that these remarks should not be taken at face value. He was a much abler teacher than his present dissatisfaction suggests.)

[7] This is a straightforward request for assistance and was met as such. Quite different from Mrs. Severn's situation, where the difficulty was in her attitudes and not in a lack of technique.

June 12. (*on telephone*)

    M. Inadequacy feelings. I want to talk to you about this some time. Why ever did I let myself in for this course?[8]

[8] The second admission needed a little prompting. Other remark spontaneous.

June 14.

    M. Compare myself with others – ought to be able to do as well, but can't. Terrible to feel unsure.

    T. Any worse since coming here?

    M. No, felt unsure for years.[9] Wouldn't ever admit it to anybody, wouldn't now. Like teaching, but feel inadequate on technique – make up on personal relationships with children. Came to course thinking I'd be able to get away with it –

    T. That you could deceive others but not yourself.

    M. – but find I can't. Didn't expect to get help with tips but hoped to get by. Others seem to do it so easily – chap I know can do all sorts, authoritarian or permissive.[10] My evening club quite different, goes easily.

    T. You like that.

    M. I like teaching too.

    T. Is organizing easier than teaching?

    M. Not necessarily. Then there's promotion – I suppose I ought to want it, but there's something to be said for staying where I'm happy.

    T. You feel you *should* want it, but aren't sure you do?

    M. No, I'm not the go-getting type – it's not simple, I want it in some ways.

    T. Perhaps for your family but not so much for yourself.

    M. Yes. . . .[11] You caught me off balance on the phone the other day – I was just wondering why I came on the course, hadn't meant to say so.

    T. Perhaps it brings feelings of inadequacy nearer the surface. . . .[12]

M. I try one sort of teaching and then another (*developed this*).

T. Have you decided to give up? Is it outside your range?[13]

M. No, I won't give up – haven't got there yet, but it's what I want to do. . . .[14]

T. Need to unbend.

M. And I thought I *was* unbending[15] (*long complaint about silliness of small girls*).

T. Masculine superiority!

M. Didn't mean to be superior.

T. But it shows attitude.

M. Helpful to get out with some of these feelings.[16] Think I'll have to join a church with a confessional! Cheerio. (*Went out quite relaxed, with a broad smile.*)

[9] The outstanding fact about this man is his honesty, even when it might be to his disadvantage – in great contrast to those who are chiefly concerned to put up a good show.

[10] Example of a naturally wider range, or window-dresser?

[11] Another honest exchange.

[12] No use pretending he *doesn't* feel inadequate – better to accept it as a fact.

[13] This decision is his and his alone; not anybody else telling him what sort of teaching he 'ought' to try.

[14] He has incorporated this as his goal. Recognizes he may not achieve it immediately.

[15] He still has a long way to go. He isn't rigid in the sense of Miss Trent, who has no intention of altering her ways – he wants to change but it isn't easy.

[16] Tone at end of interview quite different from beginning.

June 17. Seemed to want to talk. . . . Has evidently been thinking quite a bit.
Six months later, seen when back at work.

M. Didn't feel I was being got at on course – in any case I needed to be got at.[17] Am allowing much more freedom than would ever have done before – will take me about two years.[18] (*Little free work visible!*)

[17] Again very honest and objective.

[18] Acceptance of time interval (see note 5). He feels that there has been an alteration.

Several years later he felt that he had made further progress towards his goal.

The outstanding point which this record brings out is that no outside person can set goals for the individual – he and he alone can decide what 'sort of teacher' he wants to be. He has to make his own value judgement – 'this is what I want to do' (note 14) – and to incorporate it as his aim. If he does not want to do something, then no amount of external pressure will bring it about, though there may be *apparent* conformity: in his own examples, it is like the headmaster standing over the children, effective in the short run but not really, or like the man who could put on several guises (although Mr. Mersey spoke admiringly of him, it sounds as if his adoption of a teaching manner was an external response, not coming from within). It is worth making this point strongly, in view of the reported remark, 'Some of us would *like* to be directed'. Would he *really*, if it came to the test? It may be helpful here to make a clear distinction between the values, which only the teacher can decide for himself, and the means and techniques for the achievement of his goals, about which he may very properly receive direct suggestion and advice. I said in Chapter 5 that direct advice can sometimes have a boomerang effect in cutting at confidence, but in this case, where Mr. Mersey is very conscious of his limited technique, it can be helpful (very probably this is the real meaning for him of wanting to be directed – not directed as to goals, but advised as to means).

The part of the tutor was first (May 4) to clarify the issues – the choice was between working with the children or keeping them down, with encouragement to choose the former – and when Mr. Mersey had made his choice, to provide support thereafter. Notice that this support is not *merely* direct help with technique, useful though this is here; it is of greater importance to give the more subtle support involved in respecting Mr. Mersey's right to decide his own ends. For instance, there was danger in his attitude of May 30, 'I want to do what is expected'; and though it was reasonable that he was given a lead at the beginning (May 4) in making his choice, it would be another matter entirely if that external leading had continued. His own honesty and integrity would have prevented it from being satisfactory to him for long, but to begin with he was very vulnerable to outside pressure because of his own knowledge of his shortcomings in comparison with his ideals. This is a good example of the danger that supervisors may fill a felt need, for help and guidance on technique, but then may go further and attempt to lay down what 'should be' the student's goal. The more important thing is to accept people where they are now and so leave them free, as in the present example (notes 9, 10, 11), to speak frankly of their inadequacies and doubts. (Incidentally, one gets thereby a far better picture of Mr. Mersey – 'better' in two senses – than one would obtain merely from considering his present performance: if one judged him simply in terms of a preconceived standard, as is necessarily done in examining or assessing, one would miss the integrity of his attempts to widen his range.) When Mr. Mersey felt able to discuss his weak points, the tone of the tutorials became more hopeful (note 16), and at the end he himself seems in no doubt as to the genuineness of the change (note 18).

This example, like that of Mrs. Severn, shows that whereas a tutor may encourage, facilitate, and support, any genuine and lasting change in attitude must come from within. I do, however, believe that, given favourable circumstances which I have tried to indicate (strong enough motivation in the individual, a basic confidence, and outside support), quite important changes of attitude can occur.

Granted, then, the theoretical possibility of such changes, how does this affect the duties and responsibilities of the tutor? Is it his job to concern himself with aspects of his students other than their work? Some changes of attitude may seem to him desirable: is it right that he should use what influence and social skill he possesses to encourage their emergence? But, if it comes to that, who is he to give an opinion as to what is desirable or undesirable for somebody else? At what point does influence become pressure, and pressure manipulation? On the other hand, when does a narrow interpretation of his function become an abrogation of his responsibility? Where does responsibility end, and interference begin?

These and related questions raise ethical issues – of 'hidden persuaders', brainwashing, social engineering – whose full discussion goes far beyond the scope of this book. It is as well to be aware of their ramifications in order to avoid slick and over-simplified answers, and to realize that in effect we are dealing with the age-old problem of the nature and functions of the educator. Everyone must come to terms as best he can with these questions, and formulate his own ethical and philosophical principles in the light of which he will test his practice and decide how far it can be justified.* For the immediate purpose of this chapter it may be sufficient to indicate briefly a few signposts.

If I take my shoes to be mended, I expect the cobbler to do this efficiently, and I would not accept his concern for my soul as an excuse for botching my sole, even though the former is more important. Similarly, the primary duty of any teacher is to help his pupils or students in their *work*, and no high-flown claims of 'promoting all-round development' can justify neglect of this. But the analogy with the cobbler breaks down if it suggests that a clear-cut distinction can always be made between intellectual and general development: it may sometimes be necessary to pay attention to other aspects of a learner's development in order that he may make the best use of his intellectual opportunities. This is a truism with regard to children, particularly if they are young or backward, but it holds also throughout, and even at the college or university

---

* From a very different field, Mead in *Male and Female* (1949; Second Appendix) raises some extremely interesting questions which are relevant to the issues discussed here.

stage we may need to remember that we are dealing with whole persons and not with disembodied intelligences. (This has, I believe, come out very clearly in the examples I have given.) Furthermore, education is concerned not only with the development of individuals, but with their development *in society*, and hence the emphasis on techniques of adjustment; teachers, again especially of younger children, are expected not only to instruct but to encourage development in ways which society considers desirable.

There is, therefore, a double extension of what might be thought the teacher's primary responsibility – for example, to teach John Latin: he may need to think of John as a whole, and of others besides John. In the first extension the welfare of John is still the main consideration, in the second it is not. I believe that it is in these extensions that confusions arise. In the present discussion, the one that is of particular interest is the first, and the second will be omitted (with the comment that it raises issues of indoctrination, expediency, etc., which go beyond the range of my examination).

Let us assume, therefore, that John's welfare is genuinely sought. If John is a child, his teacher 'knows better' in many spheres, not only in Latin; but if John is an adult, his tutor 'knows better' only as regards his special competence, and in other respects – personal maturity, worldly experience, outside interests – the advantage may go either way. It is thus particularly difficult for a tutor of adults to claim that he is forwarding all-round development when his students are patently no more in need of his help than he is of theirs. He may then stick to his last, teach his subject or craft and leave it at that – fair enough. But if the argument of the preceding paragraphs is correct, some of his responsibility is towards his students as people and not just as examination-fodder: how then is the dilemma to be resolved?

I believe that the answer is to be sought along the lines of 'exploring with' the student, rather than in laying down solutions, which, however acceptable they may be to the tutor, are not so to the student. The tutor can help by making himself available in case of need, but it is beyond his competence to press his opinions on another. If, as was suggested in the chapter on supervision, it is often advantageous to give adults opportunities to make their own learnings (that is, even in the field where the tutor *has* a special competence), then *a fortiori* this should be so in other fields. It indicates a subtle lack of respect for other persons – for their ability to cope, for their values – if the tutor presumes to know all their answers, even if he is right, and he very well may not be. How would he like it himself? As was mentioned in Chapter 7, this simple question forms a very useful test, by which the ethical standing of his proposed course of action can be judged. It is not, of course, a final test, but if what he is doing cannot stand up even to this question, it is fairly clearly unjustified. I have already suggested that it is for Mr. Mersey, and for no one else, to decide what 'sort of teacher' he wants to be: in this example the tutor's support was helpful and not interfering. On the other hand, it was on the borderline of interference when the tutor said to Mrs. Severn, 'Wouldn't it be better if you made your own decisions . . .?' – although in that particular instance no harm was done. Perhaps the tutor was right in thinking that a change of attitude towards increased self-determination would be desirable (from the subsequent material this seems so), but the point here is that the tutor's suggestion went beyond what Mrs. Severn was at the time prepared to accept, and was therefore risky. A clear example of interference would be the proffering of unwanted advice to, say, Miss Trent.

Scrutinizing these three examples, we see that in the first Mr. Mersey was going at his own pace; in the second Mrs. Severn was being rushed a bit, but along lines she really wanted to follow; whereas the third would be a case of completely external guidance. Leaving out of account the *effectiveness* of the three procedures, and considering only their justifiability, it seems reasonable to conclude that they are ethically defensible in proportion as they are student-centred. To think that one knows what is best for other people, what changes of attitude are desirable and what undesirable, can be a form of spiritual pride. (It may be noted here that the attitude of 'Father knows best', which one meets in paternalistic systems of psychiatry, once it has accepted manipulation for the good of John, may continue to accept manipulation when it is *not* for the good of John, and pass insensibly over to the mechanistic robots of 'social engineering', that is, the second of the extensions mentioned earlier.) The best safeguard against this is entirely to renounce the temptations to play God, and to be clear that each individual, be he tutor or student, is responsible for his own life.

The difference between tutor and student is that it is part of the function of the tutor to mind about his students' welfare, whereas there is no reciprocal obligation on the students. That is, the tutor has *a* genuine responsibility to his students as people, but he has not *the* responsibility for them which is theirs alone. His duty is not to take away from their proper responsibility, but to be available to explore with them in their need and at their pace, helping them by his support and acceptance. He is then respecting the personalities of his students, as he would wish his own personality to be respected. It is salutary to remember that tutors are not repositories of infallible wisdom, and that 'changes of attitude' may be desirable in tutors no less than in students.

Chapter Ten

RELATIONSHIPS

WRITTEN WORDS suffer from the disadvantage that they are groping and indirect when they attempt to deal with matters of personal communication such as form the topics of this and the three previous chapters. Tone of voice, gesture, and facial expression, all play a part in conveying a total impression, and the actual words sound flat and dull, and may be misleading, in their written form.

For instance, a remark which looks quite harmless as far as the words are concerned, may *sound* censorious; or, as we saw in dealing with discussion, 'We won't go into that now' can look in print more directive than it is when spoken. Even the inflexion of a single word such as 'Yes' or 'No' can alter considerably the impression that is received.* For example, if a student says 'I don't feel that I'm very good at getting on with other people', this is a painful admission which should be received with respect. There is all the world of difference between 'No?' (meaning 'don't you?'), which is merely a noncommittal sign that the remark has been heard and which leaves it open to the student to continue, and an affirmative 'No' (meaning 'I agree with you'), which suggests that everybody is aware of this and which can be very discouraging. Still worse is the emphatic 'No!'

Even spoken words can be roundabout, and this is one of the

* See Compton, *Spoken English* (1941, p. 146).

reasons why expressive methods* such as role-playing or psychodrama can be so useful in teaching students, as an alternative to lecturing. 'Psychodrama can show people in a new light. When we did a little I felt it helped understanding of other people. Long afterwards some incidents will come back to give a flash into oneself' (F.S.). On one occasion, a class was considering interviewing as a means of getting information. One member was the probation officer who had called at a school to make enquiries about a boy, and another was the headmaster. The improvised conversation went along much as one might expect, until the 'headmaster' said, 'Oh, he's not a bad lad – not a bad lad at all – *I* quite like him'. The entire class laughed loudly, for the tone of voice, expansive and yet defensive, said more clearly than words could do 'The little horror!' and it was quite evident that this ambivalence had gone home† to them. It was one of the most effective small episodes I have seen, and conveyed to the hearers: (i) I'm not going to be frank with this chap; or (ii) perhaps the headmaster was deceiving himself, and was far more punitive to the boy than he realized. (iii) In either case, the reliability of the headmaster as an informant was impugned. (iv) Opinions are not evidence. (v) A wise interviewer will take into account other things besides the words spoken in forming his estimate of a situation. In a few seconds more had been conveyed to *and received by* the class than would have been possible from any lecture, because the students saw and felt the situation as a whole, and it made its impact directly. In comparison, a lecturer's description of the pitfalls of interviewing and his analysis of complex and ambivalent attitudes would have seemed laborious, roundabout, and unconvincing.‡

* Descriptions of these methods can be found in Knowlson (1951), Thelen (1954), Maxwell Jones (1952), and Klein (1961).

† Note the use of this phrase in Chapter 8.

‡ There is, of course, a case for pointing the moral afterwards, so that the intuitive and immediate grasp of the situation is linked to the students' conscious thinking, and particularly so that the overtones in points (iv) and (v) are not overlooked. See also Garrett (1942), and Sidney & Brown (1961).

Written words are still more indirect and it will be seen that the description of this incident has spread out over a long paragraph. Even so, I cannot be sure that it has made the right impact, for the key words of the headmaster may be more difficult for a reader to interpret than I realize, with auditory memory of the scene to help me. (An *oral* description would be equally lengthy but at least could mimic the intonation.)

Tape-recordings do not solve the problem because gestures and other visual indications are missing, and film, apart from the question of expense, can easily become stagy.* In any case, having chosen a book as the medium, one must make the best of it as long as one does not forget that there are serious limitations to its use in this field. 'Stage directions' of the type used in Chapter 8 can help a little; so can glosses and comments (as long as they do not make the whole too cumbrous and appear to break a butterfly on the wheel); but the best help can be found in the readiness of the reader to read imaginatively and to use his empathic powers as well as his critical apparatus. The role-playing example I have given can also show us that understanding between people is not wholly, nor perhaps mainly, a matter for the intellect, but for feeling and sympathy as well. (I use sympathy in its literal meaning of 'feeling with', not as 'feeling sorry for'.) In so far as the reader is able to imagine what it feels like to be Mrs. Severn or Mr. Mersey, his understanding of Chapters 8 and 9 will be increased; just as in the parallel situation of a tutor wondering how he can deal with his students, it will help him (as suggested in Chapter 7) if he is able in imagination to put himself in their place.

I shall now consider this faculty in more detail and particularly the limits that have to be observed. The easiest way to begin is by contrasting two imaginary extremes. Mr. A's world does not really touch those of his students and, though

---

* Experiments have been made, for instance at the University of Chicago, in the use of taped recordings of interviews for teaching purposes. Professor Rogers and his associates can thus reinforce and supplement the descriptions given in their books – but they still use books as a medium.

he instructs them conscientiously, he might as well have graven images in front of him as living people for all the difference it makes to him. His contact with them is entirely intellectual. Miss B, on the other hand, has identified so much with her students that she cannot regard them dispassionately: she takes their behaviour much too personally, is as upset by their misfortunes as if they were her own, considers it a point of honour that they should do well, and is hurt and offended if they do not. Whereas Mr. A's relationships are sharply professional and concern for the student as a person is lacking, Miss B does not distinguish between the personal and professional. It will be readily agreed that both extreme positions are undesirable, Mr. A's because he does not recognize any bond of interest or feeling, Miss B's because she does not limit it. It would be possible to present all intermediate positions on a sort of eclipse diagram, with a continuum ranging from no contact to total absorption. Most of us are somewhere in the middle.

It may be helpful here to borrow from aesthetics the concept of 'psychical distance', which was first developed, I believe, in a brilliant article by A. E. Bullough in the *British Journal of Psychology* (1912).* Bullough suggested that an experience, or a work of art, can fail for us for one of two reasons – it may be so far away that it appears remote and lifeless and we cannot work up any concern about it, or it may be so near and insistent as to be painful (our concern with it is *too* close). An aesthetic response comes midway. Regarded as a spectacle, a house on fire is beautiful and awe-inspiring: but the owner of the house is unlikely to regard it with such detachment – his immediate concern leaves no room for an experience which, to the other spectators, may be an aesthetic one. A melodrama may seem impossible and absurd to sophisticated members of the audience – they are too far away: but the sailor in the anecdote who called to the captive heroine 'Hold on, miss, I'm

* It is interesting and suggestive that the notion of 'empathy' also comes from aesthetics. Cf. Vernon Lee, *The Beautiful* (1913).

coming. I'll save you', failed to achieve aesthetic distance for the opposite reason. Similarly, a jealous husband may be quite incapable of appreciating *Othello* as a work of art, however excellent the performance he attends, because for him it is too raw and painful.

The key words in the above examples are 'concern' and 'detachment', and the tension between the two provides the distance required for an optimum aesthetic experience.

Another way of approaching this question of 'distance may be as holding a balance between the intellectual and the emotional. The attempt to understand and explain behaviour in neatly categorized terms can sometimes appear cold and blood-less, 'pinning a butterfly on a card', with the implication that there is all too much detachment and too little concern, and that once a label has been attached, there is no more to be done; yet the opposite extreme, of giving up all attempt at objective understanding, leads to a bog of unregulated emotionality, miscalled sympathy. People are not specimens and resent being treated as such, but neither do they want to be the objects of a sort of emotional slumming. True understanding involves both knowledge and feeling, not the subordination of one to the other.

Much of this discussion of distance could, I believe, be adapted to help us in our present problem, how the tutor can seek a balance between the personal and the professional. If a tutor has some concern for his students as people, his work will be more effective than that of a tutor whose remoteness repels contact; but, on the other hand, if he lacks detachment and identifies himself with one or some or all of his students too closely, the resulting loss of proportion will make him less able to help them effectively.* Some illustrations from several fields may help to clarify the distinction between personal and professional.

* See also Read, *Education through Art* (1943, p. 283), and Balint & Balint, *Psycho-therapeutic Techniques in Medicine* (1961, Chapter 10).

1. Ashdown and Brown* give an example of a client (Agnes) who was given the social worker's home telephone number 'with complete confidence that Agnes would respect her privacy in any but a genuine emergency'. The unspoken assumption is that the relationship is a strictly limited one and that the client may have free and unrestricted communication with the worker on the office phone, but outside office hours communication ceases and may be resumed only as a very special concession. Within these professional limits, however, a genuine relationship at quite a deep level can develop, but it is not the contact of personal friendship.

2. It seems to me the weakness of an otherwise excellent book, *Probation and Re-education*,† that it overlooks this point, and blurs the distinction between friendliness and friendship. The probation officer shows practical friendliness to those placed under her care, but nobody on earth can *require* her friendship – it can only be given. 'The wind bloweth where it listeth.'

3. Similar considerations arise in connection with the Cambridge-Somerville Youth Study,‡ where caseworkers (not all professional social workers) took pre-delinquent children under their wing. The growth of a *genuine* relationship cannot be legislated for, but in the last resort that is what matters. (This comment is mine, but I think it is a fair one, and helps to explain the inconclusive results of the experiment. It is a complete mystery to me that the official assessor should have made no attempt to correlate the outcome with the number of changes of 'friend' – considerable in some cases, on account of the war. She correlated almost everything that could be correlated, and yet this, which stands out a mile, was left out.)

* Ashdown & Brown (1953, p. 52).
† Glover (1949).
‡ Powers & Witmer, *An Experiment in the Prevention of Delinquency* (1951).

4. Residential nurseries are expensive because they must be staffed 24 hours a day, 365 days in the year. To provide proper relief for the professional staff is difficult and, even if this is achieved, further problems of mental health are raised. Mothers, however, do not ask for reliefs.

5. An exceptionally attractive student from overseas was worried that her male tutor had never once looked at her admiringly. It was a new experience for her, and she felt it as a rebuff. Most tutors, however, would feel that he was prudent to keep his susceptibilities apart from his work.

A professional relationship, of its nature, is limited and defined by the purposes it serves. It may be more 'expert' than the personal care it replaces, as for example in the case of the nursery or the professional friendliness of the social worker. The nurses will no doubt avoid the worst errors of ignorant parents, and social workers will continue to show tact and acceptance to even the most irritating clients, in situations where the nearest and dearest of the latter would long before have broken down into anger or tears. But this bright professionalism can sometimes appear rather hollow, a denial of the natural (though 'bad') reactions of anger or tears.* It is only because he is not personally involved (at least not on the deepest levels) that a probation officer, say, is sufficiently detached to take the longer view of his cases† – he can keep it up during his day's work and go thankfully to relax at home, where he feels he can, if necessary, snap at his wife and children. There is something to be said for the description of home as 'a place where you can behave badly' – not of course a place where you

* Compare Coleridge, 'Sybilline Leaves' –
'And he who works me good with unmoved face
Does it but half. He chills me, while he aids
My Benefactor, not my Brother Man.'

† An unstable adolescent flared at her teacher 'You're not human. I've done all I can the whole morning to make you lose your temper and you won't.' To this girl, temper would have been a reassuring sign that she could understand. It would have brought the teacher to her level, and so made her human.

do (habitually) behave badly, but where you feel easy enough to act spontaneously.

A professional social worker (and in this generic title I include tutors) is fortunate if his basic attitudes are sufficiently positive to enable him easily and naturally to get along smoothly in most ordinary situations: he will then need to use his 'professional' manner only as a sort of auxiliary engine in more difficult situations where his natural impulse would be to make a fuss. If his basic attitudes to people in general are negative, it is too hard to expect of him that he will maintain an even 'professional' demeanour, since it is under constant strain. It is probably true that a tutor cannot help people in any real sense unless he likes* and accepts them; and, conversely, unless they also like him, they will probably not accept his guidance at more than a superficial level of 'getting by'.†

A relationship which is basically sound can stand quite a bit of wear and tear, and there is no need for people to feel that they must be on their best behaviour *all* the time (if there is this feeling of tense compulsion, it probably means that the underlying attitudes are by no means as positive as they might appear). A baby prefers its scolding parents to the most hygienic nursery; the probation officer's children do not need to be told that his concern for them is on a different level from his concern for his cases, even though he is cross with them sometimes; and a tutor can make an unstudied and straightforward contact on an ordinary outgoing human level with his students. In short, naturalness keeps breaking in, and this is all to the good when it means that a tutor can act without fearing for the consequences of his spontaneous burst of irritation or rather foolish witticism. Let us hope that he feels sufficiently sure of himself and of his group to act naturally most of the time, so that he can keep his

* I mean 'liking' at an operative level and not simply in the realm of fine phrases. It is not much good feeling that you have a call to go and cure lepers if when you get there you find you do not like lepers. Duty is a colder word than liking.

† Compare also Rogers, *Client-centered Therapy* (1951; *passim*, especially Chapter 2).

professional detachment in reserve for those situations where it is really needed.

Two comments arise here: (i) he can make mistakes and still preserve an easy contact; to err is human – but (ii) it should not happen too often. I pointed out in Chapter 7 that power barriers may be stronger than a well-meaning tutor realizes. *He* may feel that he is on an easy friendly footing, but he may still be held to a formally correct standard of conduct and speech and judged accordingly, by his group. He is not one of the boys, and should not try to be.

Nevertheless, there are situations where more than natural bonhomie is required. Spontaneity may be an attractive trait, but sometimes the immediately tempting response would make matters worse. The tutor, that is, must avoid getting embroiled as a person and must exercise professional detachment, keeping out of feuds and forgoing the temptation to take things too personally. In terms of our concept of 'distance', what is too near is seen out of focus and blurred, and proportion is sacrificed. Something of this sort had happened to Mr. Humber in Chapter 7. His concern had overcome his detachment: he looked on the behaviour of his student as a personal threat, and reacted as a threatened individual and not on a professional level. I dealt with the question of authority separately because it is in this connection that difficulties are most likely to arise, but in principle other attitudes besides aggressive ones may challenge the tutor's ability to maintain steadiness and balance.

For instance, a tutor, conscious of his own good intentions, may find that it is his students' fears rather than their aggressions that are more than he can take. He may learn to stand aggressive outbursts unmoved, and still be puzzled, bothered, offended, irritated (at a personal level) by the irrationality of anyone being scared of such a patently harmless person as himself – and may unconsciously take it out of the student concerned. Or another tutor may feel that the greatest threat lies in immature fixations of the 'crush' variety. It may, however, be helpful to remember that, as regards projected emotions, the tutor is an easy target whatever the particular form the projection takes. He has no need to blame himself for the anger or fears, and equally he need not flatter himself that his virtues cause the crush. Just as there are some whose attitudes to an authority figure are immediately resentful, so there are others who tend to react to authority with undue dependence, and others still who make it into a threatening bogy. If the tutor remembers that these attitudes occur irrespective of the particular authority figure involved, his own responsibility in the matter remains the purely professional one of helping his students to the best of his ability. He will not, that is, fight the aggressive, or reject the fearful, or attempt to squash the over-dependent – as can so easily happen if one or all of these people get under his skin and so out of proportion. In a particular case, it may be a sign of progress for a student to attempt to form *any* relationship, and even if it is an unduly dependent one (for example, a crush on the tutor or another member of the group) it could be better than the previous isolation. Immature though it is, it may represent the putting-out by the personality of one small bud, and it needs to be handled with care and respect, so that it may lead to a general advance. Similarly, it may be an indication of genuine growth in another person who was formerly unable to say 'bo' to a goose that she will now stand her ground and defend herself – even if it takes the form of attacking other people.

It is useful for the tutor to ask himself 'What does this behaviour mean to this person?' and to try to see it in the light of the whole personality of which it is one partial expression. In trying to appreciate the other's point of view, I am not for one moment suggesting that the tutor should *identify* with the student. The opposite indeed is the case – his attempt to see the other side is the best antidote possible to 'Is this behaviour a threat to me?' which is the usual state of mind when the focus is blurred. Instead of concentrating on his own personal position, his interest is outwards on the other, and so his essential detachment is maintained. Put differently, his concern is genuine, but it is not a personal concern, as it would be if his own involvement were too great. For example, whereas Mr. Humber had such a heavy personal stake at issue that he did not think of how the behaviour looked to the other person, a more detached tutor, faced with a similar situation and less overwhelmed by the possible threat to himself, might have been able to resolve it altogether. He can, as we say, 'take a longer view' when his personal concern does not obsess him. It is more important to consider why a person is acting as he does than to reject the behaviour because it does not come up to general expectations (for instance in the case of immature students) or because it is a challenge to authority (as in aggressive ones).

We may now return to the question of spontaneity from a different angle, that of the student, and try to relate it to the preceding paragraph. In the long run, we behave as our underlying attitudes prompt us to, though the expression of those attitudes may be hampered by constraint, external or internal. Take, for example, a tutor like Mr. Humber who clamps down on anything that challenges his authority. That does not relieve the student's problem, it simply drives it underground. The tutor has, in fact, added his own external constraint and made it more instead of less difficult for his students to behave spontaneously. I am not advocating a free-for-all, and there are obvious limits to untrammelled 'self-expression' in a group situation, but in a private situation such as a tutorial there is something to be said for making it as easy as possible for students to talk naturally and honestly, even if it involves some element of criticism. The tutor need not agree with everything that is said, but at least he can listen to it quietly and without rushing to correct every tendentious remark. Let us suppose that Miss Eden begins by making disparaging remarks about inadequate organization. Is the criticism in fact true? The students are where the shoe pinches and the tutor may learn from their complaints: it is more important to see that the matter is put right, than to stand on one's dignity and pretend that nothing *could* be wrong. Miss Eden may then say that she does not like a certain aspect of her work, let us say the work in school (this is a personal reaction, as distinct from the factual matter of the inconvenient arrangements). The tutor's hackles may rise, if it happens to be his pride and joy (another personal reaction, but let us hope that he controls it). He cannot contradict her (for if she does not like it, she does not like it), he would be foolish to show his own irritation, so he says very little and lets her go on. By staying quiet he learns more of her point of view and, in spite of himself, becomes interested and forgets his irritation. He may add a comment or two (for *complete* silence on his part might be unnerving, because unnatural), but most of the time he lets her talk. Sooner or later she says *why* she does not like the work in school, and the admission is then common ground between them, not a matter of charge and counter-charge.

This is not an imaginary picture, though I have condensed it very much in time, but one I have seen happen over and over again. In essence, what occurs is that by not joining battle on a side issue the tutor can get a better feel of the whole. He is keeping the ring (rather than descending into it as a combatant) and so leaving Miss Eden free to come out with her opinions, and even if they are uncomplimentary or perhaps confusedly contradictory, still he is learning what those opinions are. She may not say very much – that is up to her – but at least she is not being blocked by barriers of his making (what I called the external constraints in a previous paragraph). It may be some time before she trusts him sufficiently to remove the internal constraints and to say frankly (for example) how unsure she feels,* for this is a sore subject.

* An interesting discussion of insecurity and inadequacy can be found in Plant (1950), *The Envelope*.

In the light of these considerations, let us look again at the example of Mrs. Severn. There are plenty of places, particularly at the beginning of her story, where progress could have been blocked and unprofitable blind alleys entered if a wrangle had developed on the subject of aggressive words, manner, or actions – not to mention the possibility that, as she says, she would have withdrawn altogether. Several challenges were not taken up. By keeping the ring, and figuratively keeping his distance, the tutor was able to remove external pressure. In a non-critical atmosphere it is easier for anyone to relax and be himself, and this proved true of Mrs. Severn also. She found herself able to bring to light and discuss with a second person the anxiety which was hampering her in her work, and in the process much of the internal constraint was dissipated and she could acquire a fresh perception of herself. As Mr. Mersey said, it is helpful to get out with one's feelings.

The following extract is also relevant to the issues under discussion: 'Thank you for letting me talk about things. Quite early on I noticed that I felt completely comfortable with you, so I was able to tell you things that I would not even have admitted at one time, and having fished them out and found that I could talk about my problems without feeling ashamed because you did not despise me, I shall never feel ashamed again and I am already forgetting all about it. . . . I know that you need not have listened to me, so I thank you all the more for doing so'* (F.S.). The key phrases here are 'completely comfortable' (that is, absence of external constraints *and* of inner defensiveness); 'things I would not have admitted' (compare a similar phrase of Mr. Mersey's); 'because you did not despise me' (acceptance as a person); 'I am already forgetting all about it' (troubles that have been dissolved seem less overwhelming and can sink into the background). In fact, the conversations mentioned seemed natural enough to the listener, who was

---

* I am grateful for permission to quote this. The writer of this letter has not been used as an example anywhere else in this book.

rather surprised to find, much later, from the letter, how important they had been to the speaker – a good example of differing points of view.

To conclude, a tutor can be of real help to his students in so far as (i) he is not obsessed by personal considerations; (ii) he can maintain a suitable balance between detachment and concern; (iii) he makes it easy rather than difficult for the students to consider realistically and without defensiveness their own assets and limitations. These conclusions, I think, are generally applicable. To them we may add a fourth, of more limited application. In certain circumstances, a student may have worries and anxieties which get between him and his work and which can, to some extent at least, be helped by common-sense methods. This means that the tutor is acting in a therapeutic capacity. Obviously, he is not a professional 'therapist' in the usual sense of the term and he should not attempt to dabble beyond his competence. But within his limits he can still serve a genuinely therapeutic function: to borrow a useful distinction from Slavson (1958), he does not set out *intentionally* to provide therapy, but his support and acceptance can be therapeutic in *effect*. For instance, there are better and worse ways open to lay persons to deal with manifestations of insecurity in normal adults – and it would be a pity to choose the worse. I have tried to indicate some of the considerations that should be taken into account in such a situation and that may help a tutor to adopt a policy which is not merely opportunist nor swayed by personal irritation. Steady and reasonable behaviour by the tutor can do no harm and may possibly do some good. It may be objected that the methods suggested are time-consuming, as indeed they are – but the real question is whether time wasted in fruitless wrangling over side issues could not be better spent in working on more positive lines. It is possible to be so busy as to get into a habit of dealing with everything in a hasty, snatching sort of way – when a little time taken in standing back from the problem, and in trying to discover the pattern and the principles that underlie it, would be well repaid in a more *effective* and thoughtful approach, and so would save time in the end.

It will be seen that I am not an advocate of impressionistic methods. Certainly there is a place for intuition, if by intuition is meant a holistic approach, with an emphasis on the feeling as well as the intellectual elements involved in understandings between people, but not if it is glorified guesswork. One should be ready to justify one's hunches if necessary at the bar of reason.* I would put, as the two most important qualities involved, steadiness and sensitivity – sensitivity to the position and feelings of others (all that is usually expressed as 'empathy'), and at the same time steadiness to see things in proportion. Admittedly the two qualities do not always go together, and if only one could be available (which would be a pity), of the two I would choose steadiness. At least it can do less harm and go less wildly wrong.

The ability to achieve contact with the members of his class is an important attribute of an effective teacher, at whatever level. It is not less important for a tutor of adults, for though its absence may not be dramatically reflected in discipline pro-blems, lack of contact involves a weakening of morale in the group. Very little has been written about contact, as far as I have been able to discover, in spite of its importance. In this chapter I have tried to follow some of the threads that may guide us towards its understanding. Spontaneity, an absence of posing, the ability to relax, freedom from defensiveness, unself-conscious naturalness – these are some of the words that have been bandied about. When I try to go behind them, the first thing that comes to mind is the useful distinction established by I. A. Richards (1926) between the 'stock response' and a genuine one. Contact is the very antithesis of everything associated with the stock response: it is the impact of a real

* This *can* be done. There are usually small indicants (cf. Allport & Vernon, 1933) which can be adduced, and the habit of giving evidence for one's statements is recommended.

174

experience. Is *that* why the 'bright professional manner' mentioned earlier can sometimes ring hollow – because one feels that one is meeting, not the real person, but a façade? It is a useful expedient adapted to meet a situation that otherwise would be unmanageable – it is, in fact, a sort of defence (and none the less useful for that). It may be better than the usual alternative of anger and tears, yet still be only a second best. As Ashdown and Brown* point out: 'We do not find the abstraction of a professional self very useful in our own thinking. It is what the worker is as a complete person that is brought into play in the course of personal service and behind this lies her whole personal development up to that time' – that is, the distinction between prrsonal and professional is ultimately untenable.

In the last analysis, it is what the person *is*, and not his professional skill, that matters. Here are two contrasted quotations that illustrate the same point:

> . . . *In tragic life, God wot*
> *No villain need be. Passions spin the plot*
> *We are betrayed by what is false within.*†

'Though I . . . understand all mysteries and all knowledge . . . and have not charity, I am nothing.'‡
The inner weakness that destroys, the absence of simple, unreflecting pleasure in other people (Paul's charity), cannot be compensated for by a professional persona, however glib, however impressive. Manners can be taught as an external observance of rules (Richards's stock response) but *inner* courtesy is the mark of a tranquil mind, at peace with itself and friendly to others: at the same time, manners have their uses and are better than unmannerly behaviour. Similarly, it is persons and not personae who make contact: but professional tram-lines can avoid chaos.

* Ashdown & Brown (1953, p. 151).
† Meredith, 'Modern Love'.
‡ 1 Corinthians xiii. 2.

The point is that the formalizing of behaviour (manners, professional standards, road safety codes, social conventions, rules of prosody or of counterpoint, the laws themselves) makes life simpler in that we do not have to choose anew every minute, but the price to be paid is in a lack of freshness and spontaneity, of face-to-face immediacy. 'Is this a good poem? Look in the book of rules', leads straight to the stock response. 'Were his grandparents Aryan?', 'Don't play with children from the wrong side of the tracks', 'No coaches', 'Officers only' – these stratify people on grounds of race, class, or rank. This stratification makes for orderly pigeonholes – but the achievement of sympathetic understanding across the pigeonholes is more difficult.

Controlled and distanced behaviour, as between people involved in a professional relationship, is an improvement on the jungle of 'taking things personally'; spontaneous ease, when it can be achieved, is better still. The less what I have called the auxiliary engine has to be invoked the better, but that implies tolerance and goodwill on both sides. To achieve contact there has to be a good human and not merely a good professional relationship. At the same time, contact admits of degrees and is not necessarily reciprocal.

'Be yourself' was the advice given to Peer Gynt. But if to be yourself is to be full of envy, hatred, malice, and all uncharitableness, it sounds risky advice for anyone, whether tutor or student, to adopt: had he not far better build up his professional dikes against the encroaching waves of his own unregenerate nature? The latter course is, however, a counsel of despair, and in most cases we have more to gain than to lose by following the former. I have been struck by several examples where the removal of barriers erected by pride or fear was not followed by the disastrous consequences that were anticipated when they were set up, but rather led to a general easing of tension. To stand and look one's bogys in the face (as the writer of the letter quoted earlier did) is often to discover that they were not so very terrible after all,* and in the years that have intervened since they were looked at they seem to have shrunk in size and power to appal.† This is often true of people who fear their own aggressive and destructive tendencies, and perhaps feel that they are more wicked than they are: it can be a real relief to such people when they feel free enough to be themselves. 'You must let your own experience tell you its own meaning.'‡

Ashdown and Brown, speaking of a psychiatric social worker, make a number of valuable points which could receive a wider application: She 'will not assume that she knows in advance what is good for [her client] or that it would help fundamentally in the solution of his difficulties if he were persuaded to see things from her standpoint. . . . She will see her own role as one of giving courage . . . not through persuasion and externally applied reassurance, but through the building up of a relationship between herself and the client within which he will feel confident and free enough to make his own discoveries. As a warmly interested yet disinterested and uncriticizing person, the worker can be relied upon for support. . . . She will recognize that in any such relationship a phase of dependence or hostility . . . must be accepted as a natural element. . . . There is room within this general method for work of many kinds and at many levels.'§

In other words, she keeps the ring, he makes his own discoveries (compare for example Mrs. Severn), she provides support. 'Interested yet disinterested' recalls what I have called the balance between concern and detachment. If dependence or hostility is natural then it need not cause undue alarm. Finally, the statement that this general method is capable of adaptation at different levels seems to me indubitably true

* 'It is almost uncanny how things fade out of the picture when their *raison d'être* is revealed.' Sullivan, *The Psychiatric Interview* (1955, p. 238).

† There are striking examples of this in the story of Miss Cam in Rogers's *Client-centered Therapy* (1951, p. 118 and p. 124).

‡ Rogers (1951, p. 97).

§ Ashdown & Brown (1953, p. 149). Compare also Carrington (1951), *Psychology, Religion, and Human Need*, especially Chapters 4 and 13.

Educating Older People

(compare it, for instance, with the approach of Rogers and his associates). As a summary of a helpful professional relationship it could hardly be bettered.

But – we are also people, and this is the note on which I should prefer to end. Man may be proud that he is 'dressed in a little brief authority', but it is salutary to remember that the trappings of office may be no more than the emperor's new clothes. If the person in them is not able to sustain the responsibilities of his job, he may retain power but forfeit respect. A tutor of adults is vulnerable: he cannot easily put on a show; he has little margin to spare; he may find himself constantly being stretched to the limits of his range. Since he has to live dangerously in any case, he may as well take his ease where he can, call it a day, and be himself.

Bibliography

ALLPORT, G. W. (1942). *Use of personal documents in psychological science.* New York: Social Science Research Council.

—— & VERNON, P. E. (1933). *Studies in expressive movement.* New York: Macmillan.

ARMFELT, R. (1949). *Education: new hopes and old habits.* London: Cohen & West.

ASHDOWN, M., & BROWN, S. C. (1953). *Social service and mental health.* London: Routledge & Kegan Paul.

AUER, J. J., & EWBANK, H. L. (1947). *Handbook for discussion leaders.* New York: Harper.

BADLEY, J. H. (1955). *Memories and reflections.* London: George Allen & Unwin.

BALINT, M., & BALINT, ENID (1961). *Psychotherapeutic techniques in medicine.* London: Tavistock Publications; Springfield, Ill.: C. C. Thomas.

BARZUN, J. (1953). *Teacher in America.* New York: Doubleday.

BION, W. R. (1961). *Experiences in groups.* London: Tavistock Publications; New York: Basic Books.

BOTT, ELIZABETH (1957). *Family and social network.* London: Tavistock Publications.

BULLOUGH, A. E. (1912). Psychical distance. *Brit. J. Psychol.* **5**, 87.

BUREAU OF CURRENT AFFAIRS (1950). *Discussion method.* London: Bureau of Current Affairs.

CARR-SAUNDERS, SIR A. M., MANNHEIM H., & RHODES, E. C. (1942). *Young Offenders.* London: Cambridge.

CARRINGTON, W. L. (1951). *Psychology, religion, and human need.* London: Epworth Press.

CLARK, G. K., & CLARK, E. B. (1959). *The art of lecturing.* Cambridge: Heffer.

CLEUGH, M. F. (1951). *Psychology in the service of the school.* London: Methuen.

—— (1956). The reactions of adult students to a written examination. *Brit. J. educ. Psychol.* **26**, 51.

COMPTON, J. (Ed.) (1941). *Spoken English.* London: Methuen.

179

Bibliography

COREY, S. M. (1953). *Action research to improve school practices.* New York: Teachers College, Columbia University.

D'EVELYN, K. (1954). *Individual parent teacher conferences.* New York: Teachers College, Columbia University.

DOLLARD, J. (1949). *Criteria for the life history.* New York: Peter Smith.

EPHRON, B. K. (1953). *Emotional difficulties in reading.* New York: Julian Press.

FLEMING, C. M. (1949). *The social psychology of education.* London: Routledge & Kegan Paul.

FORSTER, E. M. (1907). *The longest journey.* London: Arnold.

FROMM, E. (repr. 1955). *The fear of freedom.* London: Routledge & Kegan Paul.

—— (1949) *Man for himself.* London: Routledge & Kegan Paul.

—— (1956) *The sane society.* London: Routledge & Kegan Paul.

GABRIEL, J. (1957). *An analysis of the emotional problems of the teacher in the classroom.* Sydney: Angus & Robertson.

GARRETT, A. (1942). *Interviewing, its principles and methods.* New York: Family Service Association.

GLOVER, E. R. (1949). *Probation and re-education.* London: Routledge & Kegan Paul.

HAMILTON, G. (1946). *Principles of social case recording.* New York: Columbia University Press.

HARDING, D. W. (1941). *The impulse to dominate.* London: Allen & Unwin.

HARE, A. P. *et al* (1955). *Small groups: studies in social interaction.* New York: Knopf.

HARTOG, P., & RHODES, E. C. (1935). *An examination of examinations.* London: Macmillan.

——,—— & BURT (1942). *The marks of examiners.* London: Macmillan.

HARVARD COMMITTEE (1946). *General education in a free society.* London: Oxford University Press.

HOSLETT, S. E. (Ed.) (1946). *Human factors in management.* New York: Harper.

JERSILD, A. T. (1955). *When teachers face themselves.* New York: Teachers College, Columbia University.

KLEIN, J. (1961). *Working with groups.* London: Hutchinson.

KNOWLSON, M. S. (1951). *Informal adult education.* New York: Association Press.

LANGDON, G., & STOUT, I. W. (repr. 1955). *Teacher parent interviews.* New York: Prentice-Hall.

LEE, V. (1913). *The beautiful.* London: Cambridge University Press.

LEIGHTON, A. H. (1946). *The governing of men.* New Jersey: Princeton University Press.

MADGE, J. (1953). *The tools of social science.* London: Longmans Green.

MANSBRIDGE, A. (1944). *The kingdom of the mind.* London: Dent.

MAXWELL JONES (1952). *Social psychiatry.* London: Tavistock Publications; New York: Basic Books.

MAYO, E. (1949). *Social problems of an industrial civilization.* London: Routledge & Kegan Paul.

MEAD, M. (1949). *Male and female.* London: Gollancz.

MOBERLEY, W. (1949). *The crisis in the university.* London: S.C.M. Press.

MORENO, J. L. (1934). *Who shall survive?* Washington: Nervous and Mental Disease Pub. Co.

MUNROE, R. L. (1942). *Teaching the individual.* New York: Columbia University Press.

OFFICE OF STRATEGIC SERVICES (1950). *The assessment of men.* New York: O.S.S.

PEERS, R. (1958). *Adult education.* London: Routledge & Kegan Paul.

PERLMAN, H. H. (1957). *Social casework.* London: Cambridge University Press.

PLANT, J. S. (1950). *The envelope.* New York: Commonwealth Fund.

POWERS, E., & WITMER, H. L. (1951). *An experiment in the prevention o delinquency.* New York: Columbia University Press.

RAYBOULD, S. G. (Ed.) (1959). *Trends in English adult education.* London: Heinemann.

READ, H. (1943). *Education through art.* London: Faber.

REMMERS, H. H. (1954). *Introduction to opinion and attitude measurement.* New York: Harper.

RICHARDS, I. A. (1926). *Principles of literary criticism.* London: Routledge & Kegan Paul.

—— (1955). *Speculative instruments.* London: Routledge & Kegan Paul.

ROETHLISBERGER, F. J. (1947). *Management and morale.* Cambridge, Mass.: Harvard University Press.

—— & DICKSON, W. J. (1939). *Management and the worker.* Cambridge, Mass.: Harvard University Press.

ROGERS, C. R. (1942). *Counseling and psychotherapy.* Boston: Houghton Mifflin.

—— (1948). *Dealing with social tensions.* New York: Hinds, Hayden & Eldredge.

—— (1951). *Client-centered therapy.* Boston: Houghton Mifflin.

—— & DYMOND, ROSALIND F. (1954). *Psychotherapy and personality change.* University of Chicago Press.

Bibliography

SHARP, G. (1951). *Curriculum development as re-education of the teacher.* New York: Teachers College, Columbia University.

SHERIF, M., & SHERIF, C. W. (1953). *Groups in harmony and tension.* New York: Harper.

SHUMSKY, A. (1958). *The action research way of learning.* New York: Teachers College, Columbia University.

SIDNEY, E., & BROWN, M. (1961). *The skills of interviewing.* London: Tavistock.

SLAVSON, S. R. (Ed.) (1947). *The practice of group therapy.* London: Pushkin Press.

—— (1958). *Child-centered group guidance of parents.* New York: Int. Universities Press.

SMITH, M. B. et al. (1956). *Opinions and personality.* New York: John Wiley.

SNOW, C. P. (repr. 1954). *The masters.* London: Macmillan.

—— (repr. 1954). *The new men.* London: Macmillan.

SNYDER, W. (Ed.) (1947). *Casebook of non-directive counseling.* Boston: Houghton Mifflin.

SNYGG, D., & COMBS, A. W. (1949). *Individual behaviour.* New Hork: Harper.

STAINES, J. W. (1958). The self picture as a factor in the classroom. *Brit. J. educ. Psychol.* **28**, 97.

SULLIVAN, H. S. (1955). *The psychiatric interview.* New York: Norton; London: Tavistock Publications.

THELEN, H. A. (1954). *Dynamics of groups at work.* University of Chicago Press.

TRUSCOT, B. (1943). *Redbrick university.* London: Faber.

UTTERBACK, W. E. (1953). *Group thinking.* New York: Rinehart.

VALENTINE, C. W. (1932). *The reliability of examinations.* London: University of London Press.

—— (1938). *Examinations and the examinee.* Birmingham Printers Ltd.

WHITE, R. W. (1953). *Lives in progress.* New York: Dryden Press.

WHITEHEAD, A. N. (1955). *The aims of education.* London: Williams & Norgate.

WHYTE, W. H. (1957). *The organization man.* London: Cape; New York: Simon & Schuster, 1956.

WOOLF, M. D., & WOOLF, J. A. (1957). *Remedial reading.* New York: McGraw-Hill.

YOUNG, M., & WILLMOTT, P. (1957) *Family and kinship in east London.* London: Routledge & Kegan Paul.

Additions to Bibliography

AUERBACH, A. B. (1968). *Parents learn through discussion.* New York: Wiley.

CLEUGH, M. F. (1968). Against interpretation. *Forum,* **10**, 3.

CLEUGH, M. F. (1964). Group discussion. University of London Institute of Education *Bulletin,* New Series No. 3.

KATZ, R. L. (1963). *Empathy.* New York: Free Press of Glencoe.

MARRIS, P. (1964). *The experience of higher education.* London: Routledge.

ROGERS, C. R. (1967). *On becoming a person.* London: Constable.

ROGERS, J. (Ed.) (1969). *Teaching on equal terms.* London: B.B.C. Publications.

Index

185

Index

References to Examples